Think Like a Plant

Growing vegetables at Broadfield Court

Marion Williams

Published by Password Publishing, 64 Bargates, Leominster, Herefordshire, HR6 8EY, UK

http://www.passwordpublish.co.uk

© 2007 Marion Williams

The moral right of the author to be identified as the author of this work has been asserted.

ISBN 0 9522532 5 9
British Library Cataloguing in Publication Data
A catalogue record for this book is available from the British Library

All rights reserved. No part of this book may be reproduced, stored in an information retrieval system, transmitted in any form or by any other means – electronic, mechanical, photocopying, recording or otherwise (other than small extracts for review purposes) – without the express prior permission of the publisher or a licence permitting restricted copying in the UK issued by the UK Copyright Licensing Agency. This book may not be lent, resold, or otherwise disposed of by way of trade in any form of binding other than that in which it is published without the prior consent of the publisher.

Designed and Typeset in Aldine and Arial by Password Publishing
Cover design by Password
Printed by Henry Ling Ltd., Dorchester, Dorset, England

Photo credits: Peter Simmons, David Williams, Suzanne Spicer, Charmion Garrity, Mervyn Tong, Marion Williams.

Think like a plant

Dedicated to the memory of

Keith R H James

of Broadfield Court

June 1921 – November 2001

As a child, living in a house her father built overlooking the garden pool at Eywood near Titley, with the ruins of Eywood house, home of the Harleys, Earls of Oxford, nearby, the old kitchen gardens belonging to Eywood which had been turned into a market garden run by Mr Henry Mills, fascinated Marion and her twin, Marlane. They would often be sent to buy eggs there, and at other times, accompanied by their mother, would select fresh veg from the walled garden, which would be weighed in the potting shed on an old pair of scales. Often, the twins would be allowed to choose a flower to take home. Happy memories of these visits to a kichen garden as a child influenced Marion in her choice of career.

Marion Williams has been growing vegetables for most of her adult life and loves it. She daily provides all the vegetables for the popular Court Cafe, and also provides the house with fresh vegetables as required. She is a fervent believer in the old ways of growing food before pesticide and herbicide sprays were invented. Providing wholesome, chemical-free food for all to enjoy, her enthusiasm for her work is always apparent.

She is also a smallholder with her partner Mervyn (also a gardener) at the cottage they are renovating near Pembridge, a beautiful Herefordshire village a short drive from Broadfield Court.

The plants tell us what to do
And the weather tells us when to do it
So think like a plant
But keep an eye on the weather

Contents

Copyright	4
Dedication	5
Contents	7
Map of the garden	10-11
Introduction	13
Old surveyer's map	19
Tools	21
Sowing	25
Hardening off	27
Soil	29
Showing and exhibiting	31
Growing sweet peas	34
Growing vegetables	37
Artichokes – Jerusalem Artichokes	37
Artichokes – Globe Artichokes	38
Asparagus	39
Aubergine - egg plant	40
Beans	41
Broad	41
Runner	42
French	44
Beetroot	45
Brassicas	46
Carrots	49
Celery	51
Cucumber	51
Garlic	53

Herbs	54
Other Herbs	55
Leeks	59
Lettuce and other Salad Leaves	60
Onions	67
Peas	68
Potatoes	71
Parsnips	73
Pumpkins, Courgettes & Butternut Squash	74
Swedes	75
Spinach & Swiss Chard	76
Tomatoes	77
Pests	79
Rabbits	79
Slugs and snails	80
Mice	80
Whitefly	81
Deer	81
Seasons	82
Autumn	82
Winter	83
Spring	85
Summer	87
Recipes	89
Gardener's Hymn – *Dalonie Peel*	97
Epilogue	98

Acknowledgements

I would like to thank all the following people who have helped make this book possible

Mrs Vivienne James, owner of the Broadfield Court Estate

Anna and Sheila for encouraging me in the beginning

The Café staff for their support; Bodil, Michelle, Pam and Geraldine, with special thanks to Pam and Geraldine for the recipes.

My other helpers in the garden; David, who for 30 years has tended the grapevines, mown the lawns, trimmed the hedges, and feeds Denise the cat.

Richard for his part-time help during the growing season, and Meg who helps out in the garden as a volunteer.

Crispin Hack for drawing the map of the garden.

Peter Simmons, of Password Publishing for his help, guidance and patiently sorting out and editing the text. Brian and Lys Gable for proof reading.

Leon, who taught me all he knows about growing plants and maintaining a garden.

Su Morgan Jones, who provides essential maintance for a gardener – a massage once a month.

Daloni Peel for giving permission to use her poem 'A gardeners hymn'.

And last but not least Mervyn for suggesting the title of this book and for his support throughout.

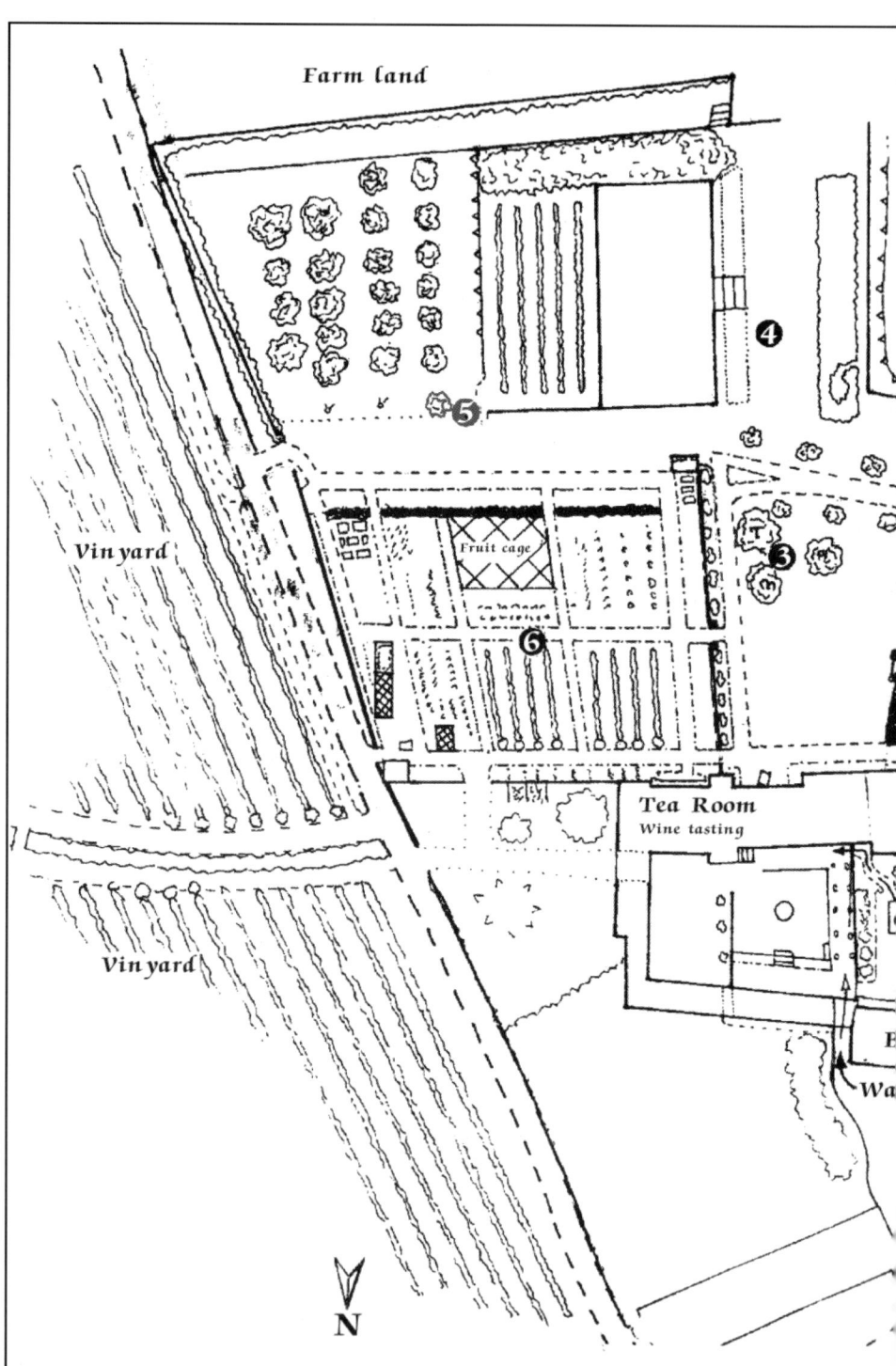

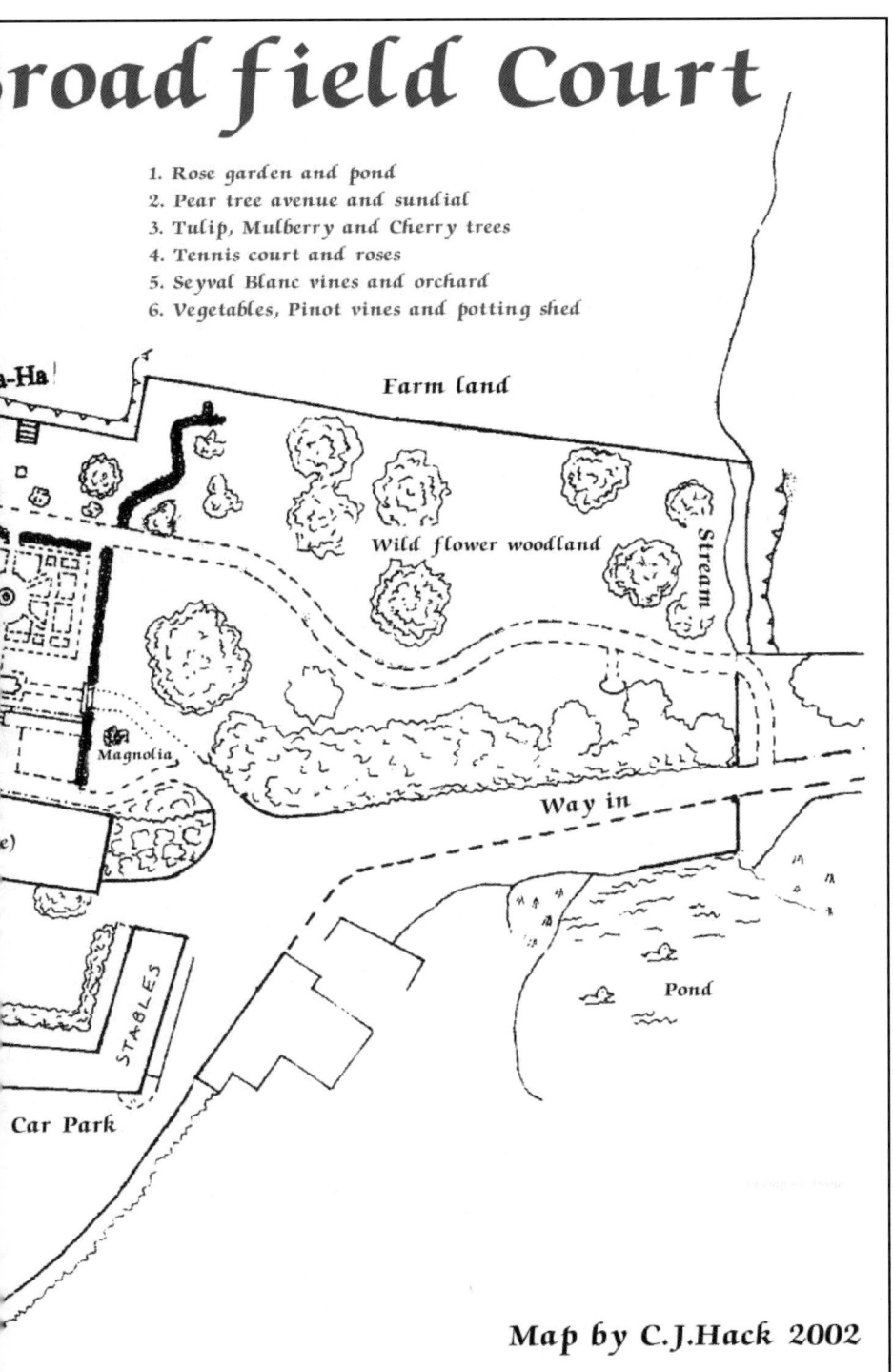

Introduction

As a child, travelling on the school bus to Lugwardine from Leominster along the country lanes near Bodenham, we would pass a black and white lodge at the entrance to a driveway lined with Horse Chestnut trees. In the spring, the grass under the trees was transformed into a yellow carpet of daffodils. I often wondered what lay beyond the trees, a grand mansion perhaps, or an empty space where a mansion used to be?

Several years later this mystery was solved when I discovered Broadfield Court at the end of the drive and started work there as a gardener. Now, my working day begins when I push open the wrought-iron gate into the garden at Broadfield Court, where I have now worked for almost thirty years, half my lifetime. A gravel path overhung with bay and holly trees leads from the gate past the ancient manor house with its six south-facing gables, each one representing a different century (there used to be eight, an Edwardian nursery wing was demolished in 1968).

The path continues towards the walled Kitchen garden where fruit trees are trained against the stone walls, each wall being a chosen site for particular trees with names such as Brown Turkey, Lord Napier, Czar and Conference, and straight rows of vegetables mingle with self-sown flowers in the red-brick edged plots. On the sheltered north wall grow the more delicate varieties; figs, peaches, nectarines and a recently-planted fan-trained apricot. At the centre of the kitchen garden there is a tall pear tree which each year produces masses of golden fruits which fall to the ground and attract colourful butterflies. I head for the heated greenhouse situated at the far corner next to the potting shed, headquarters for our garden cat, Denise, who is asleep in a plant propagating tray, and where the kettle is plugged in!

I notice the changing seasons ... sometimes the early morning sky is crisscrossed with pink vapour trails, and frost sparkles on the lawns, but on grey winter mornings the red geraniums in the greenhouse are the only bright jewels of colour to cheer me up until the snowdrops under the Copper beech tree signal the start of spring. I often think that it is better to be outside with the birds singing - how lovely it is to hear the robin's cheerful melody in

winter, or to see the leaves gradually changing their shades of green to ochre and russet red in autumn - than staring gloomily out of a window, when I can be part of it all.

When it rains, there is the smell of damp earth and each plant stands to attention with renewed vigour, the birds, refreshed, chorus with joy and you will find me in the potting shed sharpening tools and stacking discarded plant pots, with the sounds all around me, waiting for the rain to stop so I can go out and be part of it all again.

When I stand in the potting shed doorway, looking south beyond the greenhouse roof, through the branches of the oak trees, I can look beyond the undulating Herefordshire landscape over the fields, hedges and woodlands, towards Callow and Dinedor Hills, and on my left, Shucknell Hill can be seen in the distance, while nearby Longmans Hill rises above the vineyard planted on a field that slopes down to a valley where the Calderwell brook flows, hidden by trees, until it joins the River Lugg a mile away near Bodenham.

The Kitchen garden is part of four acres laid out to the south of the house, and little has changed here since a sunken garden was added (now planted with roses) in the 1920s. Lawns and flower borders are separated from the adjoining farmland by a HaHa [a wall, fence or other barrier set in a ditch to divide lands without marring the landscape].

Visitors to the garden tell me how peaceful it is and, apart from RAF jets occasionally screaming overhead, there is usually only the sound of birdsong and a distant tractor working the fields to interrupt the silence.

The weather forecast decides which jobs I can do. It is Autumn now with only the sound of rooks to disturb the silence. I collect my wheelbarrow and a rake from the potting shed, ready to clear up leaves from the lawn and start another day working here in the garden at Broadfield Court.

When I first started work in the garden (part time to begin with, March–October) my knowledge was very limited, I knew that nasturtiums were flowers and roses definitely have thorns. On my first day I arrived wearing clothes that were fashionable in

Lyston Court in its heyday

1978; bell bottom jeans, a tank top and probably platform soled boots (my outfit soon became more practical rather than fashionable). I was introduced to Mr Cooke the head gardener, who wore a shirt and tie and his lace up boots were polished, he insisted that I call him Leon and not Mr Cooke. My first task was in the fruit cage where I was shown how to tie the raspberry canes to supporting wires using a reef knot.

Leon had learned to be a gardener in the traditional way, starting out as a garden boy aged 14 at Lyston Court in south Herefordshire (the house has now been converted into flats). One of his first jobs was to rake the gravel drive every morning to keep weeds from growing, the prospect of doing this daily chore would almost reduce him to tears. Life was tough for a young gardener; other jobs included washing terracotta flower pots and wooden seed trays in cold water, clearing up weeds, raking up fallen leaves, and using a besom broom to sweep worm casts off the lawns. But he stuck at it because he knew that all these difficult tasks were part of his early training.

After years of hard work he came to Broadfield Court in 1960 to live with his family in the lodge at the top of the drive. At first, I wasn't allowed to do any skilled work, Leon would edge the lawns with hand shears and I would rake up the clippings. I was shown how to use a dutch hoe and can remember being asked to 'edge by the 'edge', south Herefordshire dialect for cutting the lawn edge next to the yew hedge with hand shears and clearing up afterwards. I did a lot of clearing up. I also discovered that every full wheelbarrow had to be pushed uphill to the compost heap. One of the most tedious jobs was picking off strawberry flowers.

After the vineyard had been planted in a field next to the Kitchen garden (the farm staff dug the holes and we planted each vine with a spade), strawberry plants were planted in between the rows of grapevines as a catch crop. The rows were very long (the lengh of the field) and my job was to remove every flower from each plant in May so that the plants would fruit later on in August and September, as the strawberries sold for a higher price later in the season. I soon got backache bending over the plants, until I discovered that if I sat down in between the strawberry rows and shuffled along backwards, blissfilly listening to my transistor radio to relieve the boredom and wearing a pair of shorts, I could save my back and get a good suntan on the front of my legs better than if I was standing upright.

For fifteen years I watched and learned until eventually Leon handed me a packet of seeds to sow by myself, my training was complete.

All this may sound harsh by today's standards, but I was interested enough to keep going. In other words, if you couldn't stick the work, you weren't fit to be a gardener. Leon also gave me three pieces of advice; always have a sharp knife, some string and a nail in your pocket (it used to include two bob for a phone call, but now we have mobile phones) and always keep back some plants after planting the rest out, just in case.

Leon retired in 1997, but he still works half a day once a week. I now have the responsibility of the parsnips that won't germinate, and all the other responsibilities of running a large garden.

The garden, covering four acres, is part of a large estate of a thousand acres, which the late, sadly missed, Keith James and his wife Vivienne bought from the Romilly family in 1968. Mr James had the foresight to plant the vineyard and therefore to employ me. The Estate is now run with the help of their children and grandchildren. There are two farms, a large herd of dairy cows, pheasant shoots, and a tourist trade that has evolved over the years.

Broadfield Court history

Broadfield is mentioned in the Domesday book of 1086. The house as it exists today is an interesting mixture of architectural styles dating from the fourteenth century, a pointed gothic window overlooks the rose garden and the main entrance from the courtyard has ball flower mouldings. A Tudor fireplace in the dining room was uncovered by William Helme revealing the letters H de B set in a wreath and a date 1216, the initials were thought to belong to Hugh de Brad felde the owner at that time who gave his name to the estate.

John Henry Burchall purchased Broadfield Court in about 1825 when the house was described as being in a dilapidated state. He had married Katherine Cooke in 1803, the daughter of William Cooke a director of the Bank of England. John Burchall subsequently converted Broadfield from a farmhouse to the Gothic manor house seen today, complete with gargoles and gables. Susanna Jane, their only child, married William Helme a Cotswold wool merchant and they had four sons; Burchall (1836–1893), Cuthbert (1837–1870, William John (1842–?) and Harold (1849–1896). After her husband died in 1851 aged 53, Susanna moved

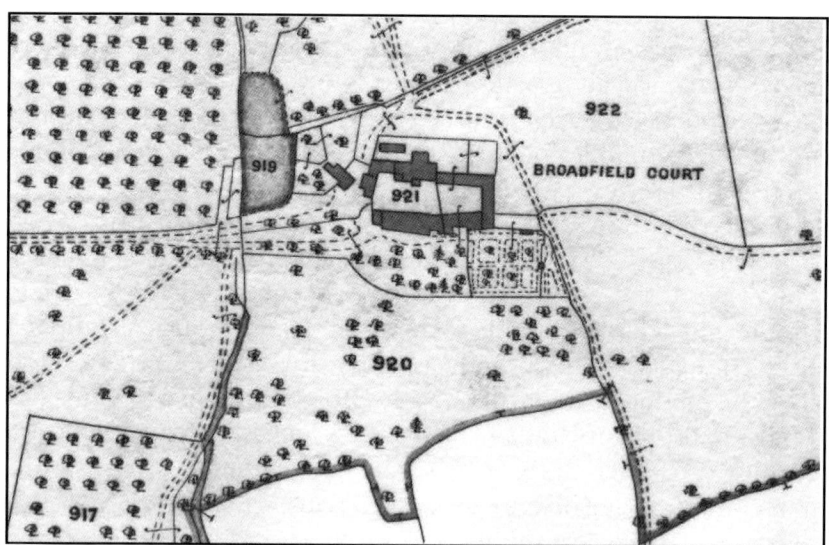

Detail from surveyer's map of 1904 showing Broadfield Court buildings and walled garden

her family from Stroud (Glos.) to live with her father at Broadfield Court (he died in 1863 aged 86). She outlived three of her sons when she died in 1904 aged 96, the surviving son, William John, married Marianne Haywood in 1869, but she died ten years later aged 35 and there is no record of any children. He remained at Broadfield after his mothers death .The census of 1881 lists Susanna Helme as head of the household, farming 420 acres of land, also William John, widower aged 38, daughter-in-law Laura Helme, widowed wife of Cuthbert (he died aged 33), a housekeeper, cook, palour maid, housemaid, and Henry Evans aged 14 described as a boy of all work.

In the early 1900s, William John increased the estate when he bought some of the surrounding land and buildings from the Arkwright family of nearby Hampton Court, including Lower Broadfield and Riffins Mill. In 1919 the estate was sold to Frederic Carnegie Romilly (1886–1953) second son of Samuel H Romilly (1849–1940) who lived at Huntington Park near Kington, and great grandson of Sir Samuel Romilly Solicitor General and legal reformer (1757–1818).

Frederic Romilly added more land to the estate and remodelled the garden in the Arts and Crafts style that was fashionable at that time. After he died, his son Simon inherited Broadfield Court Estate and sold it to the James family in 1968.

When I first started work here, the farm covered most of the running costs just by working the land, now marquees are erected on the lawn for summer weddings, and times have changed; tourists wander in what was once a private garden, and a cafe has been opened to provide meals all year round. The menu dictates what I have to grow, and the produce has to be fresh and interesting to look at all at the same time.

The estate gardener has for years been just a figure in the background pushing a wheelbarrow, but what perhaps isn't realized is that he or she has a wonderful knowledge of how to grow plants, a knowledge that could be forgotten if it isn't shared with a new generation of gardeners, this is my opportunity to pass on that knowledge learned in the traditional way at Broadfield Court.

The tools all stowed away in the potting shed

Tools

All the hand tools we use in the garden are stored in the potting shed. They are familiar friends with handles worn smooth and shiny from use.

After each one is used it is put back in its usual place, the long handled hoes, rakes etc. are hung up on nails hammered into a board attached to the back stone wall of the shed, the spades and forks lean against the wall underneath. During the busiest time of the (growing) year I confess that they are put away uncleaned, but if it rains and I seek refuge in the dry, I get out the oil rag and sharpening stone. The Dutch hoes have their edges sharpened so that they can glide through the soil, secateurs are cleaned and sterilized to help stop the spread of fungal deseases, rough edges are rubbed off the spades, and my penknife has its blade honed on the stone step leading to the vineyard, the step worn smooth,

like the tool handles, from previous gardeners also using it to sharpen their pocket knives.

At the turn of the year every garden tool is given a special clean; wooden handles are rubbed with linseed oil, tines and blades wiped with engine oil. They then start the new year clean and ready for action.

One of the most important lessons I learned from Leon is to always put all the garden tools away after use, this not only helps preserve wooden handles, but saves the frustration of trying to remember where you last used a trowel, spade or fork.

List of garden tools used in the kitchen garden:

Spade – I use a border spade, a smaller version of the usual size spade
Fork - I also have a border fork
Dutch hoe
Draw hoe - including a curf
Iron rake

Dibber

Garden line

Trowel

Small hand fork

Boards – these are used when picking up weeds

Secateurs

Watering can

Young broad beans

Besides veg, flowers are also grown

Sowing

Plants need warmth and moisture to germinate, enough nutrients to encourage healthy growth, soil fine enough for root development, and a dedicated gardener with enough time to look after them! Nature is a wonderful thing, patches of bare soil are quickly covered with green plants (usually weeds) when the sun warms the soil and rain provides just the right amount of moisture. I am constantly cheating nature, by starting plants into growth artificially in the warmth of the greenhouse.

Some seeds need more warmth than others to persuade them to grow, these include tomatoes, aubergines and courgettes, so they have to be started off in a heated propagator. Other plants are started off with less heat, but they need the protection of the greenhouse to prevent them from being eaten by rabbits or slugs. I can also get a head start with broad beans and lettuce, and potato tubers are put into the greenhouse to encourage early shoots to form so that I can plant them out at the beginning of March.

The main seed order usually arrives in January, with enough multipurpose compost to last for a year, forty bags. This is a cheaper way of buying compost, and it is delivered directly to the garden.

Always having a bag ready for use in the potting shed gives the compost a chance to warm up before it is used, but if the weather is very cold, a bag in the heated greenhouse is a good idea. Most of the vegetable seed is sown directly into soil, but quite a few varieties are sown into plant modules, trays or plastic plant pots. All the containers are washed after use and stacked away ready for next time.

Sowing seeds
A plant module is placed on the potting shed bench where it is filled with compost to the brim. A second module is used to press down the compost in the previously filled one, and the filled module is

then taken outside where it is thoroughly watered and left to drain. A small dip is made in each planting space with a finger, it is quite fiddly to sow one seed in each space, and I often end up with three or four, but these can be thinned out later on. I then shake dry compost over the seeds using a fine garden sieve, until all the seeds are covered, write a label to identify the variety, and carry the module into the greenhouse and place it on the greenhouse staging covering it with a pane of clean glass, and, if the seed packet says so, a sheet of newspaper to exclude light. The most important thing then is to regularly turn the glass over to stop the seeds getting too damp, and I must check to see when they have germinated, because as soon as they do, the newspaper and glass must be removed. Lettuce seeds germinate very quickly, usually within 7-12 days, so it is easy to make the mistake of letting the seedlings become leggy from lack of light. But if that happens all is not lost, most seedlings can be transplanted into another tray of compost, planting them deeper helps, and the seedlings should grow on normally. I use the same procedure to sow seeds in trays, but I firm the compost with a square wooden tamper that Leon made years ago and which is still in use. The seeds are scattered on top of the soaked compost, and again covered with enough sieved compost to just cover them. When sowing into pots it's usually with bigger seeds, so they just get pushed into the compost before the pots are placed in the propagator.

Sowing directly into the soil

Some vegetable seeds that are not as vunerable to slug damage or not as tempting to mice are sown directly into the soil in a seed drill; a straight furrow made in the soil to the required length depending on how many seeds are to be sown. The soil is raked to a fine tilth using an iron rake, resembling fine grains of corn. I use a garden line to mark out the row and keep it straight, the back of the iron rake is used to scrape out the drill before the seeds are shaken evenly out of the seed packet along it. I have always used my feet to mark the spaces between rows, luckily my boots measure 12 inches. The row is marked at both ends with a short length of cane, but no labels unless it's an unusual variety, because they never stay put. If the soil is very dry, watering the drill before sowing helps the seeds to germinate.

Hardening off

When all the seeds that I have sown are growing strongly and happily in their seed trays in the greenhouse, they have to be gradually introduced to outside temperatures, otherwise it would be like going outside without your coat on!

Each tray or plant module is put into the cold frame which is closed at night and left open during the day. By then the days are getting longer, and it is soon time for the plants to be planted out into their final positions where they will grow until ready to be harvested.

Cold Frames next to the green house

Soil

If I dig down a spit and a half (one and a half spade depth) through the top layer of soil in the kitchen garden, the true colour of the soil is revealed, red clay. This is more noticeable when the surrounding fields are ploughed as it matches the russet red coats of the native Herefordshire cattle.

The earliest record I can find about the kitchen garden is an OS map of 1888, which means that since Victorian times the soil has been transformed with years of double digging and many wheelbarrows of muck spread over it to get the crumbly texture I am lucky to have now.

Land-drains have been put in to take away any excess moisture, but there are patches that still remain wet and sticky. Underneath the walls, the soil gets dry, but warms up quickly, making this a good place to plant early crops such as potatoes and broad beans. The height of the walls creates shady areas as the sun moves around during the day. Water is provided from a natural source on the estate and pumped to a resevoir, the dairy cows are the first on the list to be supplied with water, then the café, the house, and last of all the garden. In the summer I have turned on the tap to find that all I have is a tiny trickle of water, the supply has been directed elsewhere. So I have to be economical with the water, and try to mulch as many plants as possible. Lawn clippings are useful for this task, to keep the plants from drying out during the hot summer months.

I can grow most types of vegetables because the soil is neutral (ph5-6). Everything is grown without chemicals, the exception is if I am in dire trouble when caterpillars have stripped all the cabbage plants. All the vegetables are set out in straight rows to make them easier to grow and harvest. The soil is regularly hoed to stop it cracking during dry spells, and rotavated when each area is cleared of vegetables. Certain areas where root crops are grown, are dug over during the winter or autumn when it is dry enough to do so. There is a plentiful supply of muck provided from the farm, which is spread over the soil (this is a good way of keeping warm in the winter), and it is either rotavated or dug into the soil. Digging is another good way of keeping warm, it takes skill and practice to dig properly. Frost breaks down the soil, so that all that's needed is a rake to level it for planting in the Spring. Rotating the crops is important, every year a different area is used for growing each crop, except for the early potatoes which are always grown in a border under the north wall, so far with no ill effects.

Over the years the soil has been changed from clay to loam using lots of muscle power. Later on, artificial fertilizers were an easy option, as were chemical sprays. It is a challenge to grow produce using the traditional methods that were used when this garden first existed. I enjoy growing plants that taste wonderful, look good, are healthy, and are harvested fresh for people to eat.

Showing and exhibiting

Showing

I started with a vase of nine sweet peas, there was a class for nine stems without leaves at my local Pembridge show, and I asked Leon to help me choose the most suitable ones to cut. He chose nine perfect blooms with four open flowers on each stem. Leon had won many prizes at his gardening club show and advised me on how to 'stage' flowers and vegetables, and also how to interpret the rules written in the horticultural section of my show schedule.

I was surprised and delighted to win a first prize with the sweetpeas, of course this encouraged me to have another go at exhibiting, and the following year I entered five onions in a class, only to be disappointed when I was disqualified. I hadn't read the rules properly, I was supposed to trim the roots off the onions, this taught me a lesson, and now I carefully read through the schedule the night before the show.

For me, showing vegetables and flowers adds a different dimension to growing them. All the flowers look pretty in profusion, and I know that the vegetables taste good to eat, but quality is what counts on the show bench and the challenge is not about growing the longest carrot or a gigantic cabbage, but trying to match five unblemished potatoes or trying to find three identical runner beans.

Exhibiting

I was lucky to have Leon to advise me on how to choose, prepare and stage my exhibits, and a visit to several horticultural tents at local agricultural shows gave me an idea of what the judges were looking for and what the competition was like.

The first step was to get a schedule for the horticultural section at Pembridge show, so that I could decide in which classes I wanted to compete. I then had to buy enough white paper plates (large and small ones) to display my vegetables on. Leon loaned me his green painted exhibition vases for the flowers, and I filled each one with soaked *oasis* to help keep the flowers fresh in the hot marquee. To stage the onions, I selected five matching black plastic flower pots, washed them and filled each one with enough clean gravel to stop them toppling over, and placed an onion in each pot making sure that they were trimmed but not skinned as the schedule instructed. Shallots have to be displayed on red dry sand on a china plate to support the combined weight of the sand and onion. I try and prepare everything the night before the show, often staying up late to make sure that everything is done correctly. The next morning I load my car at an early hour ready to give myself plenty of time to set everything out on the show

Kelsae onions

benches and double check that I have put six beans on a plate and remembered to label all the herbs. I am usually exhausted by the time everything has been set out for the show judge, and drive home for a reviving cup of tea.

The most nerve-wracking part is returning to the show ground in the afternoon to see who the prize winners are. Last year I bumped into Leon and his wife before going into the show tent, he has a wry sense of humour and asked me if I had a large tin of metal polish at home, and when I looked at the prizewinners' cups I found out why, I was amazed to find that I had won the most points overall in the flower and vegetable sections. These cups now stand proudly on my mantlepiece and I am looking forward to trying to win them back again at next year's show. I think that it is important to support these traditional local gatherings where everyone can enjoy themselves, meeting up with neighbours and old friends, having a flutter on the trotting races, eating an icecream, and buying yet another plant for the garden. Showing produce isn't about trying to grow the longest carrot or the biggest cabbage, its about keeping tradition alive.

Cups won at the Pembridge show

Growing sweet peas

Sweet peas have a special place in the kitchen garden. Before garage forecourts and Interflora existed, cut flowers were as important for decoration in the 'big house' as vegetables were for eating. Leon showed me how to grow sweet peas on a cordon system. This method of growing them is quite labour intensive, but is worth all the effort because we get large straight-stemmed flowers, ideal for cutting. And of course the perfume, such a lovely powerful fragrance makes growing them even more worthwhile. I choose pastel coloured varieties because they are my favourites.

Cultivation

The seeds are sown into individual plant pots during February.

Young sweet pea plants growing strong in the greenhouse

We used to have a few special terracotta pots known as 'long toms', traditionally used for growing sweetpeas, but sadly I only have one of these pots left now. Instead I use ordinary plastic plant pots deep enough to allow plenty of room for the roots to grow. Two seeds are sown in each pot. Another nice thing about sweet peas is that they germinate quite quickly, but I am careful to place the pots in the greenhouse next to where Denise the cat sleeps, otherwise they would be taken away and eaten by a mouse! Soon, two plants appear in each pot and the strongest one has to be selected and the weakest thrown away. When the weather improves, all the pots of sweet peas are moved into the cold frame, so that they can gradually get used to the outside temperatures. The next step is to pinch back the growing tip of each plant to two leaves.

Meanwhile, during the winter months, I prepared a trench, a spit and a half deep (one and a half spades depth), the clay subsoil is broken up with a fork and I keep warm on frosty mornings filling the trench with several wheelbarrows of well rotted manure. All the soil that has been taken out of the trench has to be put back in on top of the muck, another good way of keeping warm. The worms and frost are then left to do the rest of the hard work so that when ready to plant out in April, there's a lovely deep bed of rich moist soil to put them into. The sweet pea seedlings are planted about nine inches apart and long bamboo canes are pushed into the soil next to each plant (they grow six feet tall), usually in two parallel rows. The canes are tied to wires (this is when I have to remember how to tie a reef knot), the end of each wire is wound onto a 'T' construction using long posts and a cross piece, a useful, movable structure that Leon made years ago. Each sweet pea plant is watered as soon as they are planted to get them settled into the soil, and when they are about a foot tall, they have to be tied to the canes in a special way, which takes us to the next stage.

Cordon training

I recently discovered that cordon training was first used for growing sweet peas in 1911, and we still use this method to grow them. As they grow, they are tied to the supporting canes (using a reef knot again), a pair of scissors used to cut off all the tendrils, and the side shoots or laterals are pinched out just like growing tomatoes. Regularly picked to prevent them from going to seed, they would otherwise think it is time to stop flowering. Eventually the sweetpeas reach the top of the canes. I usually let Leon do the next step, layering them, as I am not as careful or experenced as he is, and I always manage to break a stem.

Layering Sweet peas

To prolong the flowering time for sweet peas, they can be layered. Midway through the summer (depending on when I have planted the sweet peas and the weather conditions) the main growing stems that have been tied to the canes will have grown, so that by now they will have reached the top of the canes, all the flowers will have been picked, and there is nothing to tie the stems to. Layering is a way of using up the excess main stems which are taken down and started again at the base of each cane so that they end up being twice as long. The used up, non-flowering, part of the main stems are laid out horizontally on the ground and about a foot of the ends are tied to canes further along the row so that they produce flowers all over again.

Step 1: Five sweetpea main growing stems at a time are untied from the canes, the string being cut with a knife or scissors.
Step 2: The stems are carefully lowered to the ground and laid out sideways, being careful not to break any of them.
Step 3: Each stem is retied to another cane further along the row, then sideshoots (lateral shoots) are removed as before, and the stems tied in (attached to a support) as they grow back up the canes. I give them a feed high in potash which will help them produce more flowers, and they should go on flowering until Autumn.

Varieties grown
Horizon mixed and **Bouquet mixed**

Growing vegetables

Artichokes – Jerusalem Artichokes

Once you have planted Jerusalem artichokes you have them for life! Our patch is over forty years old and has stayed in a space measuring about six feet by six without straying. They grow to six to eight feet tall and they could be useful as a windbreak or to hide unsightly objects, but they only have foliage to do this during the summer months. Jerusalem artichokes die back in winter, and have to be cut back to ground level. Underneath the top foliage are the edible 'roots', these are knobbly in shape and are not easy to peel, washing them like new potatoes is easier, my mother used to roast them with the Sunday joint, and they tasted like sweet potatoes.

They can be harvested from autumn onwards. I carefully dig up the artichokes with a fork, trying not to damage the tubers and making sure that at the end of the season there are enough tubers left in the ground to continue growing for next year. Jerusalem artichokes are easy to look after, I have never earthed them up, as, unlike potatoes, they don't go green when exposed to daylight. They must be back in fashion because they are now available in my seed catologue.

Planting is best done in spring when the tubers are dormant. They are planted 5 inches deep in soil that is free from periennial weeds, in rows about 15 to 18 inches apart. The patch in the Kitchen garden is well established and happy where it is without interferance from me. I just dig what I need and leave the rest to grow as they wish, who knows, the same patch of Jerusalem Artichokes could still be in the same place in another forty years' time.

Variety grown
There is a new variety available called **Fuseau**, it has smoother tubers that are easier to peel

Artichokes – Globe artichoke

Allow plenty of space for these majestic plants,when mature they are three feet tall and just as wide.I have one specimen growing next to the fruit cage on a patch of ground that was always difficult to cultivate, because the soil lies wet here.I cut them down to ground level before the first frosts and cover them with straw or use the cut off leaves for protection,mulching around the base of the plants also helps protect them, I lost two plants during a very hard winter.

    I think that Globe Artichokes are well worth growing,because the grey green foliage is so differant from all the other plants in the garden, left to go to seed the flowers are very attractive to bees and a wonderful shade of blue.

Sowing

Easily grown from seed, the large seeds are sown in a shallow plant pot in February or March and started off in the heated greenhouse. I have to wait until the danger of frost has passed before planting them out, usually at the end of May.

Water the young plants until they are established, and mark where they are planted with a cane, it takes a couple of years for the plants to reach their full size and if you don't want to eat the globes these plants are still interesting to look at.

Variety grown
Emerald

Asparagus

For planting, I use a large draw hoe, a line for marking rows, and a spade.

There are two short rows of asparagus next to the fruit cage, they have always been there.

A few spears appear each spring, but not enough to be useful, so I decided to plant two more rows. The plants when they arrived looked like strange sea creatures, they were, in fact, the dormant roots, called crowns.

To plant them I made two straight ridges by earthing up the existing soil and adding more good loam, making the ridges about a foot high. The roots were then spread over the top of the ridged soil, I put more soil on top and firmed it by patting it flat with my spade, this helps to stop the fresh soil being washed away when it rains. It is important to make sure that the soil where asparagus is planted is completely free of periennial weeds because they are difficult to dig out after planting.

Once planted, asparagus is remarkably trouble free, the top foliage can be cut back when it turns yellow in the Autumn, although I like to leave the foliage for as long as possible as it is very useful with cut flowers and lasts a long time in water. During the winter I mulch the asparagus by spreading well rotted muck over the mounds which helps prevent annual weeds from seeding. In the Spring I am rewarded with lovely fresh asparagus spears.

Variety grown
Dariana

Aubergine – egg plant

Most of the vegetables we grow have been tried and tested over the years, but Leon never grew Aubergines, so I am still experimenting. My first attempt was growing a couple of plants in the heated greenhouse, they did produce a few purple fruits, but the plants were covered in white fly. I put some plants in large pots outside against the shelter of the greenhouse wall and all I got was one aubergine fruit. I have now decided to try and think about what sort of conditions these plants need to grow well; water, warmth and somewhere where whitefly can be controlled by natural predators, the answer is outside planted directly into the soil in a sheltered place.

I sow the seeds in January or February into a shallow plant pot, and place the pot in a heated plant propagator (we have two, so that the cat doesn't lose any sleep) being sure to put the cover on the propagator. When the seeds have germinated I remove the pot to the greenhouse staging and after about a month transplant them to bigger pots. These plants are not frost hardy so they can only be planted out after all danger of frost is over, here it is usually after the end of May. The area where they are going to be planted should be prepared in advance with a quantity of manure dug in to help retain moisture. I test the soil outside by picking up a handful, and if the soil feels comfortably warm in my hand, it's time to plant out my young aubergines. I gently tap each pot to loosen the roots, dig a hole with a trowel, firm the plants in with my hands, and give them a thorough watering – not an overhead spray, but I aim the watering can or hose at the roots and count to ten. I leave the plants to soak up the moisture overnight and if they are happy they will look as if they are standing to attention. A cane is used to support each plant as it grows. Once established, I pick out the growing tops to make them branch out, feed them with a high potash liquid fertilizer which will help them to produce the purple fruits, weed them regularly or mulch them with straw or lawn clippings to deter weeds and retain moisture during a hot summer.

Variety grown
Bonica F1

Beans

I grow three types of beans: *Broad – Runner – French*

Broad beans

Mid November, the leaves are falling, it's cold and the skies are grey, this is the time to liven things up and grow some Broad beans. I choose a variety that is suitable for autumn sowing, the Sutton is a short variety that doesn't need staking. Aquadulce Claudia is a taller variety that does need staking.

To avoid mice eating the seed, I sow mine in a deep box, twice the depth of an ordinary seed tray, so that the roots have plenty of room to develop. This is put into the heated greenhouse as close as possible to the cat's sleeping place, anywhere else and the seeds soon disappear, tell-tale signs that a mouse has taken the seed are small holes in the compost. About two weeks after sowing the young bean shoots should appear.

Hardening the plants off in a cold frame to get them used to the outside temperatures, I plant them out on a frost-free day when the soil is dry enough to stand on, spacing each plant 9 inches apart in the row and 24 inches between the rows. The taller varieties need to have canes and string to support them as they grow. I also reserve a few plants (remembering Leon's advice) because slugs can nip the stems at ground level. Black fly isn't usually a problem when broad beans are grown this early. Pinching the tops of the plants out when they are in full flower encourages more pods, and mulching between the plants keeps the weeds away. During February I sow more beans so that I have plentiful supply for Mrs James, who loves Broad beans, she freezes most of them so that she can enjoy eating them for most of the summer.

Varieties grown
Autumn sowing – **The Sutton** or **Aquedulce Claudia**
Spring sowing – **Dreadnought, Express** or **Imperial Green Longpod**

Runner beans

There is no point in starting these tender plants off before the danger of frost has passed. This is usually the end of May. The runner beans are then sown into compost in a deep box and put into the now not-so-cold greenhouse to germinate. When the plants are strong enough I plant them out next to the sweet peas. They also have a long cane as support and they will soon scramble up the canes. I experiment with different varieties with different coloured flowers. Moisture is very important to keep the beans cropping consistently and constant picking also helps. Usually, a temporary chicken wire fence is necessary as a barrier against rabbits.

Instead of planting beans in a row, it can be more interesting to plant them in a circle using canes or hazel sticks to make a teepee shape. The only drawback using this method is trying to reach into the middle to pull out weeds. You can overcome this problem by making a doorway in, and then you can use it as a place to hide if you want ... and pick beans at the same time!

The Runner Beans are grown next to the sweet peas, on top of a filled-in trench that has been prepared during the winter. The 2 foot wide trench has had several wheelbarrows of muck tipped into it, so that it has a 6 inch layer of muck at the bottom, this will help retain any moisture during the dry days of summer. All the soil that has been dug out of the trench is shovelled back in on top of the muck, and worms do the rest of the work, breaking down the muck and mixing it with the soil, so that when it is time for me to plant out the Sweet peas in April and later on (when there is no danger of frost) the Runner Beans at the beginning of June, I have a lovely mixture of fine crumbly soil to plant into. It is important to make sure that both these crops are planted within easy reach of a tap because they will need plenty of water to help them produce lots of beans and sweetpea flowers. The Runner beans also like to be sprayed over with water either in the early morning or late afternoon when the strong sunshine is less likely to scorch the leaves (water droplets magnify the sun's rays and can burn the leaves). It's easier to push 8ft long canes into the soil before the runner beans are planted out. I position the canes about 12 inches apart, and then tie them onto two overhead wires that are attached at the ends of the rows to supporting posts as for the sweetpeas, then I just plant alongside each cane. Runner beans usually twine themselves around each cane, but sometimes one or two of the plants are a bit naughty and will refuse to do this, so string has to be used to tie them to the canes. When the runner beans have just been planted out, the young leaves are very tempting to slugs and snails, and to give some protection I surround the whole area where the beans are planted, (this also works with sweet peas) with a continuous line of unpainted copper piping, making sure that the pipe touches the ground so that the slugs and snails cannot get underneath, apparently the copper gives them a mild electric shock! When the runner bean plants are mature they are no longer of interest to hungry slugs and snails, and the copper pipe can then be moved to protect another crop.

Sowing

I sow the runner beans in a deep 'orange box' lined with a black dustbin bag and with a few holes punched in the bag to allow for water drainage. The box is filled with multipurpose compost and the seeds are pushed into the compost about an inch below the surface. The box has to be put into the heated greenhouse so that the cat can stop mice eating the seed. Runner beans soon germinate in the greenhouse, and I harden them off in a cold frame when each plant has two strong leaves. They are planted out as soon as all danger of frost is over, 12 inches apart, 15 inches between rows. (Sweet peas growing next to Runner beans attract bees which help pollinate the Runner bean flowers)

Varieties grown
Painted Lady which has pretty bicoloured red and white flowers, or **Galaxy,** a stringless variety.
White swan (white flowers) and **Red rum** (red flowers).

French beans

I have grown both climbing and dwarf French beans, but I prefer the dwarf variety because they are easier to grow. The climbing ones need some protection from cold winds when they are first planted out, though an advantage is that I don't have to bend to pick them. There is a lovely variety of dwarf French bean called Purple Teepee which is a real showstopper, visitors to the garden ask me what variety it is after they have stopped to admire it! The advantage of growing them is that I can sow and plant out a row later on in the Summer. July is a good time, after most of the other garden crops have grown, these beans are ideal to fill any space I have spare in the Kitchen Garden, and they don't need canes to support them.

Sowing

Sometimes I take a risk (hoping the mice have other things to eat) and sow them directly into the soil 9 inches apart. I usually sow two rows two feet apart, pushing the seed 2 inches deep into well tilled soil. They may need protection from slugs and snails, but I find that the soil is dryer later on in the season so that I can hoe around the beans with a dutch hoe to keep the soil crumbly, which deters slugs and snails (they prefer smooth wet soil to move around on). French Beans are ready to pick when the pods are about four inches long and snap easily .

Varieties grown
Dwarf French Bean – **Purple Tepee** – dark purple pods.
Purple Queen – the purple pods turn green when cooked
Climbing French Bean – **Cobra** – grown exactly as Runner beans

Beetroot

Light sandy soil is recommended for growing beetroot. Here at Broadfield Court, the soil is loam over clay, and they seem to grow well as long as the area they are planted in has been dug over in the winter, and no fresh muck added. I look out for stones because any obstacles in the soil will produce forked beets. They are grown as a dual purpose crop, not only can the roots be used in the summer as a colourful and tasty addition to salads, but at the end of July I sow a short row, and only the leaves are picked, as, when young, the leaves are sweet and provide an interesting addition to a winter salad combined with endive and lambs lettuce. The young leaves can also be cooked and taste like spinach.

Beetroot is a trouble-free crop to grow. Occasionally aphids attack the leaves in summer, but I usually have some fine specimens not only for eating but to take to my local show.

I remember during my early days working in the garden, helping Leon to pull up beetroot left over from the summer crop, the leaves were twisted off to about 3 inches, any surplus soil was carefully washed off so as not to damage the beets. We made a heap of red sand in a room that is now part of the new café (I think it could have been the original potting shed because there were nails knocked into the walls, perhaps for hanging up tools). The beetroots were stacked in the damp sand and covered over. Later on in the winter, if the ground was frozen, which it usually was then, they would be taken by Leon into the house as a winter vegetable.

It is important to remember to be careful with the hoe when weeding this crop because the skins are easily damaged, they don't usually need watering, although a very dry, hot summer may turn them woody, but if they are used fairly quickly this doesn't seem to be a problem for me.

Sowing

The seeds are sown in mid March when the soil feels warm.

As for most seeds the soil is raked to a fine tilth, and a line is used to keep the row straight. I try to remember to sow the seed thinly because each seed will grow into three seedlings. I sow the seeds three quarters of an inch deep and five inches between each row.

I don't thin out the seedlings because I pull them as soon as they reach the size of a golf ball the remaining plants fill up the spaces in the row.

Varieties grown
I stick with the traditional ones **Detroit** and **Boltardy**.

Brassicas

This is a collective term for Brussels Sprouts, Curly Kale, Purple Sprouting Brocolli, Cauliflowers and Cabbages.

Because the café is open all the year round, not just for the main tourist season, I have to grow enough 'greens' to last from October to March or until the menu changes depending on the weather. Each year the brassica patch is moved to another area in the Kitchen Garden to avoid such things as cabbage root fly and the dreaded club root. A large area is chosen because sprouts and purple sprouting broccoli need a lot of space to grow.

From the seed catalogue I select all the varieties that will give me a continuous supply until the Broad Beans are ready to take over. I also choose varieties that are interesting to look at, such as red curley kale, savoy cabbage, and sometimes red brussel sprouts. Leeks planted next to a row of dark red curly kale is an interesting combination.

Preparation

These seeds have to be started off in a nursey bed. I usually choose the base of a demolished greenhouse as it is in a sunny, sheltered spot, and is raised up with protective brick walls providing a rabbit proof area. The seeds are sown in mid March or early April or I have sown them later on in May. Later sowing and planting out works well now that we seem to be having drier summers, sometimes there is more rain to help the plants grow later on in the season.

The soil where the seeds are to be sown is sprinkled with a little blood, fish and bone meal, and fluffed up with a fork, and then I sow the seeds half an inch deep and leave a space the length of my foot (12 inches) between each short row. I have to label each row because I still have trouble telling the difference between cabbages and sprouts, but if I lose a label Leon helps me out with identifying the plants. When the first green leaves appear I watch out for signs of flea beetle damage, little holes appear in the leaves and the crop can have its growth severly checked. Covering with fleece helps, or I have to resort to spraying. Soon the healthy young plants have to be lifted ready to be transplanted.

Planting Out

Before planting the brassicas out into their winter bed, the soil is sprinkled with pelleted chicken manure which is rotavated in.

The next job is to surround the whole planting area with a chicken wire fence held in place with canes threaded through the

wire and into the ground. I have to remember to leave a 'gateway' in the fence, otherwise, trying to climb over can result in catching your foot in the wire and ending up looking at the sky through a framework of green sprout leaves.

Rabbits and pigeons appreciate having a ready supply of green leaves, so I have to put up two forms of protection. The first is the fence against rabbits, then a quantity of baling twine has to be stretched and criss-crossed over all the plants, looking as if someone has gone mad with a washing line. I carry the brassica plants in a bucket with water in the bottom to stop them drying out too much, and I only lift as many as I can immediately plant.

Planting a large area is quite a daunting task, so it is nice to have some help. A line is used to mark each row, and the plants are laid along the line roughly in the position they are to be planted. If the soil is damp, a dibber is ideal to make a hole deep enough to cover the roots and some of the stem, firming each one into the soil with a heel completes the task. A trowel is used if the soil is dry, I hold the trowl with its back to the line, which is how I was taught to keep plants in a straight line. We used to practice this a lot while planting long rows of strawberries. You firm each plant in with your hands, planting distances are 2 feet apart for the big ones like sprouts, kale and purple sprouting broccoli, about a foot apart for cabbages. The dibber or trowel can help measure the distances if you measure it first. Each plant is watered in using a hosepipe counting to ten at each plant.

It's a good idea to plan ahead around the weather forecast, and a rainfall the next day or so helps give the plants a good start, but I watch out for sudden wilting as, despite being watered, this could be a sign of cabbage root fly damage. Fortunately, because I rotate the crop every year, I have only once had trouble with root fly, and then just a few plants were affected. Leon was unable to grow any brassica plants in his own garden because the soil was affected with club root, luckily, so far I haven't had this problem.

My biggest worry is the cabbage white butterfly. They look so lovely fluttering around the garden but the caterpillars can completely destroy the whole brassica crop, so this is one of the few times that I resort to a bug killer.

Do not worry if, like me, you either forget or delay putting string over the brassica patch, and you find next morning all the lovely young leaves stripped by pigeons. As I found out, all is not lost as long as there is a remaining growing tip, the plants will recover and grow into fine specimens.

All the string and wire can be removed when the brassicas have fully grown, and are then no longer a sweet temptation to rabbits, but if the weather gets very cold, pigeons will be tempted, especially if there is little else for them to eat. Then the string has to be put back, this time with a few canes to tie the ends to.

Leon used to randomly test the newly planted brassicas by trying to pull a plant out of the soil. If he couldn't pull one up, I had planted them properly!

Varieties grown
Brussels sprout – **Peer gynt** this variety has been available for over a hundred years and is my favourite, and a newer variety, **Millenium** and **Red Delicious** has dark red sprouts
Savoy – **January King, Ormskirk**
Cabbage – **Golden Acre, Tundra, Puma**
Spring cabbage – **Offenham Flower of Spring** (these are sown later in July–August
Purple sprouting broccoli – **Late** and **Early**
Curly Kale – **Redbore** and (green) **Reflex**
Cauliflower – **Astral f1, Mayflower** this is sown in February
Calabrese – **Typhoon**
And some years if there is space, red cabbage because it looks nice

Carrots

Carrots need the same soil preparation as parsnips, stone-free soil and no fresh muck, so that they can grow long and straight. A row is usually sown next to the onions, because apparently the smell of onions masks the smell of carrots and helps keep carrot-root fly from damaging the crop.

There are now several carrot varieties that are resistant to root fly, these are worth a try.

I usually sow the seed sparingly in the row because I don't thin them out when they have grown, as any disturbance attracts root fly, so I just pull them as they are needed when the carrots have reached full size.

Sowing

Carrot seed should be sown half an inch deep, and for a long time I had trouble growing them because I wasn't skilled enough to make a seed drill with a rake. I used a short cane instead and I didn't make the drill deep enough. After several failures and head scratching moments, I asked Leon to sow a row of carrot seed for me so that I could watch how he did it. He also watered the drill first because the soil was dry at that time and of course his row germinated evenly – it takes a lot of practice to shake seed down a row evenly, I'm still practising!

As soon as the carrots have germinated they have to be protected from hungry rabbits with a lengh of chicken wire bent to form an arc over the row. If I have the time I try and earth the carrots up with soil so that the tops don't turn green which spoils the look of the crop. We don't have the room to grow a lot of carrots, so all the ones that are grown are used in the café during the season.

We used to store the surplus in the pre café days and I can remember digging them up a row at a time, which is harder work than just pulling a few at a time, washing the soil off each carrot, letting them dry, cutting the tops off, then laying them in red sand in a part of the winery where the kitchen now is, which used to be the only frost-free area to store them. Those days are gone now, but it must have been essential to be able to store all root crops before electricity and supermarkets. Carrots fresh from the garden tastes as proper carrots should, very carroty!

Varieties grown
Parano f1 which is resistant to carrot fly
Maestro and **Rocket**

Celery

When Leon worked for the Romillys the previous owners of Broadfield he grew celery for Winter use, but didn't mention to the new owners that he could grow it because it meant a lot of work. I had never tasted home grown celery, so I asked Leon to show me how to grow the ones that need to be blanched. We prepared a small trench and I had to look through several seed catalogues before I found the right variety. The seeds are sown in a tray exactly like onion or leek seed, and when the seedlings are the size of a pencil they are transplanted to the prepared trench, planted 12 inches apart and left to grow. When the plants are 12 inches high we wrap each stalk with thin cardboard tied in place with string. I keep earthing up the plants with soil until the end of the summer, and the celery is ready to harvest in the Autumn. I couldn't wait to taste some, and it does taste so much fresher than the celery bought from a supermarket.

The main problem I have is from slug damage, which is difficult to prevent without using chemicals, but celery doesn't have to be perfect to use either as a cooked vegetable or as soup, so I can settle for a little damage and prefer to avoid the chemicals.

Variety grown
Giant Red which is frost hardy

Cucumber

Leon used to grow the cucumbers in our second greenhouse, which is unheated, on a straw bale which was buried in the soil. A large hole had to be dug inside the greenhouse to bury the bale and then it was soaked with water before being covered with fine soil and the cucumber plants planted on top. The idea was to keep the roots as moist as possible, and this does work. I have grown them using this method several times. Another method, which means less digging, and sometimes I prefer an easier option, is to make a mound of well rotted muck mixed with lawn clippings, and some fine soil put on top to plant into.

Sowing

Cucumbers need a high temperature to germinate, so I start the seeds into growth in a heated propagator. I use a wide two inch deep plant pot filled with multi-purpose compost and soaked with water before sowing. The seeds are pushed into the moist compost then it's placed in the propagator with the lid on. It doesn't seem to matter which way up the seed is placed, and it doesn't take long for the first leaves to appear (3 to 5 days). The young plants now have to be carefully nursed until the first mature leaves have grown. Sometimes young cucumber plants keel over and die for no apparent reason, Leon and I have often puzzled over a sick plant, and I have saved the odd one by carefully earthing up some compost around the stem and new roots have grown.

These plants are very tender so can only be planted out after all danger of frost is over. They need an outside temperature of 60 degrees before I can tranfer them to the unheated greenhouse, and the plants should be looking strong and healthy with good root growth at this stage. They really need high humidity and higher temperatures than tomatoes, but because I don't have the space in the heated greenhouse,they have to share with the tomatoes, so I plant them at the back furthest away from the door. Several long canes are pushed into the soil to support the plants and they are tied to the canes as they grow. To keep them producing good sized fruits, regular watering is essential, and feeding with potash also helps. Cucumbers must be picked as soon as they are ready otherwise the plant thinks that it has produced all it can and refuses to continue. Most cucumber plants that are available now are usually all female varieties, so I don't have to pinch out the unproductive male flowers. Female flowers have a miniature cucumber behind them, male flowers have just a thin stalk.

It is very difficult to grow two matching cucumbers, and I have only once achieved this. I managed to grow two fine specimens, I talked to them, and carefully watered and fed them so that they would be ready for the Pembridge show. The day before the show

I arrived at work to find that one of my prize cucumbers was missing, someone must have fancied a cucumber sandwich! I hope they enjoyed it.

Varieties grown
Palermo and **Pepinex,** both all female varieties.

Garlic

Garlic is really a perennial, but is grown as an annual. It is also classed as a herb, but doesn't look like other herbs, which is all very confusing. Garlic cloves are planted every year as early as possible, it is traditionally planted on the shortest day of the year and harvested on the longest day. I have to wait until the seed order arrives at the end of January before I can plant mine.

Planting

Garlic arrives as a bulb from the supplier. Before it can be planted the outer skin is peeled off to reveal several sections called cloves, and each one will grow into a new garlic bulb, hopefully the same size as the one started off with. A line is marked out in previously rotavated soil which has been levelled with an iron rake, each clove is then pushed into the soil just below the surface, spacing them four inches apart, six inches between rows. It's important to make sure that the garlic cloves are planted the right way up, with the blunt end down, this is where the roots will sprout from. I mark both ends of each row with a short length of cane so that I don't forget where I planted them. Garlic is usually easy to grow as long as it has enough moisture in the ground to develop some nice fat bulbs.

Home grown garlic has the freshest taste and smell, much better than any you can buy. The garlic bulbs are harvested on a nice hot day in July and dried in the sun. The bulbs are put in a wooden tray and stored in a frost-free place ready for use.

Varieties grown
Solent White

Herbs

Part of my daily routine is a parady of the old days when the gardener would call at the kitchen door, cap in hand, to ask the cook which vegetables were needed from the garden for that day's menu. Every morning (except weekends of course) I call at the café kitchen door to ask Geraldine or Pam what they would like from the garden, and they always ask me to include parsley, even in the winter, though we do have several different varieties of herbs in two herb beds. Growing in them are sage, marjoram, fennel, thyme and lovage, and also dotted around the garden are herbs grown for their interesting foliage and to attract bees. These include hyssop, lavender and chives, and we even have a bay tree growing in a sheltered place near the house, but parsley is definitely top of the list, followed by chives and mint. The mint stubbornly refuses to grow anywhere else except under the north wall in the kitchen garden.

Most of the herbs are perennials, so all I have to do is cut them back to ground level in the autumn, though lovage dies back naturally. The annual herbs I grow are parsley and basil, dill because I like it's smell, and sometimes I grow coriander, but it easily runs to seed.

Growing parsley

Parsley – Moss curled and Flat leaved – sometimes it's recommended to soak the parsley seed before sowing, this is because the seeds can take nearly a month to germinate (when sown directly outside) and soaking gives them a head start. Chitting the seed on damp kitchen paper also hastens germination. My method is to sow the seeds without soaking them into a plant module where the compost has already beeen soaked in water and allowed to drain. After sowing the parsley seed, the module is placed in the greenhouse where the warmth will help to encourage germination. The parsley plants can stay happily growing in the plant modules until the soil is warm outside and all danger of frost is over. The little plants need warmth to grow properly so that when the first frost arrives they are mature and well adjusted to outside temperatures.

Parsley needs a sheltered spot, and good crumbly soil to grow well. I plant a couple of short rows of moss curled parsley in a border underneath the west wall, which gets the morning sun and is shaded in the afternoon. It is near the path so is easy to reach when it is picked. I also grow three plants in a cold frame as insurance in case of a severe winter. The moss curled parsley plants are spaced about six inches apart and a foot between rows. The flat leaved parsley grows bigger and needs a little more space, so is planted about nine inches apart and a foot and a half between rows. The flat leaved varieties seem to be able to tolerate cold weather, they also tend to self-seed, which is a bonus because I find young plants growing in places they have chosen, where they seem to grow better than in my planned rows. Pam and Geraldine freeze some of the parsley just in case, as no one can predict the weather that far ahead. So one way or another we make sure that there is a supply of parsley all year round.

Other Herbs

Here is a list of the other herbs that are grown in the garden, and a brief description of their care and propagation.

Sage, purple – trimmed back in Spring, frost may otherwise damage it. Easily grown from cuttings, has lovely blue flower spikes when mature.
Sage, variegated – more tender than purple, I must take care when cutting back, as being too vigorous with secateurs will upset it.
Mint, common – also known as Spearmint, likes to choose it's own place to grow, move it and it will sulk. Not as vigorous or invasive as ...
Bowles mint – which has furry leaves, both are easy to grow from cuttings. If mint gets mildew in summer I cut it back to ground level and it will soon shoot again. During the winter months I cut

it down anyway, so that we have fresh growth in the spring.

Lovage – we have a plant growing under a yew hedge which has been there, happily growing in semi shade for over thirty years. Very pungent, the smell clings to your fingers. Easy to grow from collected seed, difficult from cuttings. Will die back naturally in the winter, remerging in the spring. The young seedlings look just like cow parsley.

Borage – self seeds everywhere and can be a nuisance, but easy to hoe off. Has pretty blue flowers.

Chives – once established, lasts for many years, can be split up for new plants or grown from seed. Dies back naturally in winter, has pretty purple flowers.

Calendula – pot marigold. It self seeds in the kitchen garden and flowers even in the depth of winter. It is interesting to add petals to salads.

Fennel, bronze and green – feathery leaves, attractive among flowers, self seeds and dies back naturally in winter, lovely aniseed smell.

Lemon balm – can be split up for more plants, interesting to grow among other plants for its perfume.

Lemon verbena – small shrub, stronger lemon perfume than lemon balm, slightly tender, cut back in spring, easy to grow from cuttings.

Marjoram – two varieties in the garden, one is low growing and easy to control, I cut it back if necessary, the other type could be oregano, it self seeds everywhere and is cut back in the autumn.

Rosemary – can be trimmed to make an interesting small shrub, evergreen with small blue flowers.

Thyme – small bushy plant that can be trimmed back if it spreads too far, long lasting once established.

Sweet bay – can be 'scorched' by cold winds in winter, otherwise trouble free. I trim it into shape in spring, the cuttings take a long time to grow, but are worth the effort as bay trees are expensive to buy.

Hyssop – grown as an edging plant, can be cut hard back in winter and is less temperamental than lavender but not as tall. Lovely blue flowers and perfume, cuttings grow easily.

Lavender – I don't cut into old wood, just lightly trim off the old flower stalks and keep in shape. Easily grown from cuttings and some varieties from seed, grows best in a hot sunny spot on well drained soil.
Sorrel – self seeding member of the dock family, I plant it where it can be controlled.

Basil

Basil is a tender annual, perhaps that is why I sometimes have trouble growing it!

But each year I persevere and manage to grow a few plants for the kitchen. I also grow a small pot for myself which I keep in the greenhouse so that I can nibble a few leaves with my sandwiches. Basil is supposed to aid digestion, maybe that's why I like it so much.

I have no trouble germinating the seed, it's the aftercare that I tend to neglect, this is because basil needs to be regularly watered to keep it growing well. Because this plant comes from southern India, there is no point in planting it outside until late May or when there is no danger of frost or cold winds. I have discovered that the best place to plant it is in a deep wooden trough at the end of the dismantled greenhouse, the remaining brick base providing some shelter. Basil likes a sunny spot, so this is the ideal place and I can just reach to the trough with a hosepipe, so, when I remember, it does get watered every day. The trough is filled with multipurpose compost mixed with some fine soil. The leaves are picked when needed but not all stripped off at once, and any flowers are removed as soon as they appear.

Growing Basil

I sow the seed into a small tray (to fit into the propagater), as they need a temperature of at least 60o F to germinate. This takes a while, so I have to be patient. When the seedlings have produced two leaves, I prick them out into small individual pots, keep them in the greenhouse until the plants look sturdy, then harden them off gradually in the cold frame. When the temperature outside is warm enough for me to be wearing shorts and a tee shirt, I plant them out in the wooden trough where they will be ready to be picked, and the fresh green leaves can be sprinkled over salads and sliced tomatoes.

Varieties grown
Sweet basil and **red basil** – the dark leaves of red basil are an interesting contrast.

Dill and Coriander

Both these herbs are annuals and they are easy to grow outside, sown directly in the soil, but I wait until there is no danger of frost before sowing.

Dill has an individual flavour which goes very well with fish, and the feathery green-blue foliage makes an interesting contrast among the other herbs. The foliage is used in a special fish cake recipe, a popular dish on the café menu. Dill also produces seeds that, if they are left on the plant until they turn purplish brown, can be harvested at the end of the season and used for pickling. On warm afternoons I often make a detour past the row of dill so that I can sniff the leaves, the smell is quite uplifting, especially on a hot day.

Coriander looks just like flat-leaved parsley until you rub the leaves, then you discover that it has a quite different smell. The leaves are used when they are young and fresh to decorate chilled soups, and also as one of the ingredients for a delicious mixed herb salad.

Coriander and Dill both like a sunny spot to grow in, the seeds are large and easy to handle, and they both germinate quite quickly, but run to seed easily so I sow seed from April to June because I need a continuous supply.

Leeks

Leeks are easy to grow and are one of the crops that remain in the Kitchen Garden throughout the Winter, planted next to rows of red curly kale (Redbore)they look quite decorative with their grey green narrow leaves.If one or two leeks are left to go to seed they produce a globe shaped flower,paler in colour,but the same as the alliums growing in the herbaceous border.

Sowing and Planting

Leeks can be started off in the same way as onions that are grown from seed, they are sown in a seed tray filled with multipurpose compost and placed on the staging in the warm greenhouse to aid germination.When the young leaves are the size of a pencil the leeks can be planted outside in the soil in April or May, after they have been hardened off in the cold frame.

The area where they are to be planted is sprinkled with pelleted chicken manure before it is rotavated.Each row is marked out with a garden line the rows should be 12 inches apart Using a draw hoe a 6 inch deep furrow is made in the soil for every row of leeks, (this is just like making a deep seed drill) The easiest way to plant leeks is to use a dibber or to save bending a long metal rod or bar can be used (I use a metal support from a gazebo that blew down in a gale)Make a 6 inch deep hole in the furrow for each leek, spacing them 9 inches apart,drop a leek plant into each prepared hole and fill them with water to settle the roots .During dry spells the leeks need plenty of water, the furrows they are planted in can be used as an irrigation channel .Leek stems can be blanched by earthing up the stems once the plants are established.A favourite way they are used in the cafe' is for Leek and potato soup, just what is needed on a cold winters day !

Varieties grown
Mussel burgh – a tried and tested favourite
Toledo – a late season variety
Pancho – an early maturing variety

Lettuce and other salad leaves

I grow a lot of lettuce, but not all at the same time! Lettuce is used in the café throughout the year; during the summer it is used in sandwiches, as a garnish, and mixed with herbs in a special Broadfield salad. During the winter, less lettuce is used, but I still grow a few of a variety that can withstand cooler temperatures and less sunlight. Combined with red radicchio and pale green endive and a few young beetroot leaves, I have the ingredients for a winter salad.

The time to start sowing outside is when the soil is the correct temperature. I usually pick up a handful, and, if it feels pleasantly warm in the palm of my hand, I know that the seeds will germinate. The daffodils in the orchard will be in full bloom and will be encouraging me to begin. Not all lettuce is sown directly in the soil to give them a good start. I sow some lettuce which is not classified as winter lettuce, and normally would not be sown till later in warmer weather, in plant modules as well. This works well with the traditional varieties such as Little Gem, and it gives them a chance to grow into stronger plants in the greenhouse so that when they have been hardened off (depending on the weather), they can resist slug and snail attacks. This is because their bigger leaves probably don't taste as sweet as newly germinated shoots. I also have some unusual help. I have two extra helpers, a hen and a cockerel that are allowed the run of the garden and seem to clear up most of the slug and snail eggs. They do, however, insist that they come into the greenhouse during our break times and eat the crusts from our sandwiches. I also then have to protect some of the lettuce from being pecked. This seems a small price to pay.

Pest patrol

Summer lettuce

There are so many varieties of summer lettuce that I am spoilt for choice. The cut and come again, or picking, lettuce is top of my list, and is easy to grow. I sow the seed directly into the soil, it germinates quickly, doesn't need thinning out and lives up to its name. I can pick a good supply from a row for about six weeks. Traditional lettuce, shaped like cabbages and called Butterhead lettuce in the seed catalogues, grows to full size faster then a crisphead type such as Iceberg. For this reason I only grow a few crisphead lettuce. Cos lettuce is somewhere in the middle, not as fast to mature as the traditional type, but there is nothing like a home-grown Little Gem lettuce. My favourite of all is a loose-leafed variety that can be picked a few leaves at a time, it is the darkest red lettuce I have ever seen, called Bijou.

Sowing and planting summer lettuce

Most of the Summer lettuces are sown in plant modules and grown on in the greenhouse before they are planted outside when the soil has warmed up, usually at the beginning of April. I use a trowel to plant them, spacing the lettuce plants 9 inches apart and 12 inches between the rows. First of all, the garden line is set out to keep the row straight, each plant is carefully removed from the module and placed out along the line, before they are planted with the trowel. A hose pipe is used to water them in before some chicken wire is bent over the row to protect the lettuce from being nibbled by rabbits (and our chicken).

Cut and come again lettuce such as Lollo Rossa and Bijou are sown directly into the soil. A seed drill is made in a straight line ½ an inch deep, the seeds are evenly sprinkled along the seed drill before the soil is raked back over them using an iron rake. Each end of the row is marked with a short length of cane, if the soil is very dry the drill is watered before the seeds are sown into it. The lettuce rows are hoed with a Dutch hoe to prevent the soil cracking, preferably on a hot sunny day because the sun will kill off the weeds. If lettuces are thinned out from a row and replanted, a good way of shading them from the sun and to stop them wilting after watering them, is to place an upturned plant pot over each plant, the pots can be removed once the lettuce plants have revived. Lettuce is one of the easiest crops to grow (despite the rabbits), it takes 7 to 12 days for the seeds to germinate, and about 2 months from sowing to harvest. Soon I will be rewarded with a crop of lovely fresh lettuce to keep the café supplied during the summer months.

Winter lettuce

These lettuces look and taste just the same as the traditional summer ones but they are specially bred to grow slowly during the dark winter months. In August or September I usually sow a small quantity of seed in a module, enough to provide me with two rows of lettuce which will be planted inside the cold greenhouse. After most of the other plants in the garden have died back ready for their winter rest I have the lovely sight of some bright green seedlings in the greenhouse. When the young winter lettuce are first planted out I water them in, then I carefully monitor how much water they need, because they do grow very slowly, reaching full size in February. They don't need the same amount of water as lettuce grown during the warmer months of the year, if I give them too much water they will rot, and it would be a pity to lose this important crop of Winter lettuce.

Varieties Grown
Summer lettuce – cabbage-shaped **Tom Thumb** (small and sweet)
      Unrivalled (fast maturing lettuce & Leon's favourite)
Cos lettuce – **Little Gem**
Loose leaf lettuce or cut and come again – **Leaf Lettuce** (a mixture of) **Bijou** (dark red), **Lollo Rossa** (dark copper red)
      Red Salad Bowl (red)
Winter Lettuce – **Arctic King, Rosetta**

Other salad leaves

To accompany the different coloured lettuce and liven up the salads, I grow various types of salad leaves. These include:

Endive

Endive seeds are sown at the same time as the Winter lettuce, but once the plants are strong enough, I plant them outside in the Kitchen garden, you are supposed to tie the plants up in a bunch to blanch them, this makes the leaves more tender to eat, but I have found that if I try and blanch endive, the plants rot off in the centre. I just cut the paler green leaves at the centre of the plants as they are needed, endive seems to be resilient to cold weather and a small amount of leaves can be harvested all winter.

Radicchio

Radicchio is sown in August or September, planted outside directly in the soil next to the Endive, it is the same colour and shape as a red cabbage, but doesn't grow as big. If there is a hard frost, only the outer leaves are damaged, these are the red bits that are in a supermarket bag of mixed salad.

Rocket

The main problem with growing rocket is flea beetle, which make tiny holes in the leaves, making the crop unusable in salads. I thought Leon had gone bonkers when I witnessed him holding a wooden board over the top of some young cabbage plants (which also get damaged by flea bectle), but he explained that if you smear the board with thick engine grease and move it horizontally over a vulnerable crop, the flea beetles will stick to the grease and can be scraped off and disposed of. This does work, but if the weather remains hot and the soil is dry, ideal conditions for flea beetles, they keep coming back!

My remedy is to either sow rocket seeds later in the season when the flea beetles have gone away, or sow some rocket seeds under cover in the greenhouse which confuses them. Otherwise Rocket is easy to grow.

Sorrel

There are two types of Sorrel, both are easy to grow. Buckler sorrel has light green leaves with silver patches, it can be cooked like spinach, but I grow it as an addition to salads as the leaves have a sharp taste, and there is also a broad-leaved variety that looks like dock leaves. I also grow a variety that has red veined leaves, but I don't know which variety it is because the plants were given to me. Now I have a row of them, they tend to spread if not kept under control, but they are interesting to look at, and it's nice to have something unusual in the Kitchen garden.

Corn salad or Lambs lettuce

These low-growing plants look like a miniature form of spinach, the leaves are winter hardy. I can sow Corn salad outside to accompany Endive and Radiccio, it sometimes suffers from mildew during the winter months, but is worth growing because it has interesting shaped leaves as a contrast to the other winter salad crops.

Pot marigolds

Pot Marigolds or Calendula, seed themselves everywhere among the vegetables adding some lovely bright yellow and orange colours, they flower well into (and sometimes all) winter, depending on how much frost we have. I pick the flowers so that the petals can be sprinkled onto salads for extra taste, interest and colour.

Nasturtiums

In the cold greenhouse there is a patch of nasturtiums growing among the tomatoes, they got there by accident and now I can't get rid of them because each year they produce hundreds of seeds which are almost impossible to pick up from the soil. Fortunately a fashion has started for adding flowers to salads so they come in useful. The leaves have a peppery taste. The first frost of the season kills all the nasturtium plants but they grow back the following year from the fallen seeds.

The author relaxing with her dog Shona after an exhausting day in the garden

Onions

The first seeds sown in the new year, usually at the beginning of January, are a variety of onion called Kelsae, this variety is special and the seeds have to be sown early so that they have plenty of time to grow to a mammoth size ready for my local show at the end of July, where I hope to win a prize with them. Although Kelsae is bred for the show bench, they also have a good flavour and, I am told, don't make you cry when peeled.

All the other onions grown are started off as sets, the ground where they are to be planted is prepared during the winter, muck is incorporated into the soil either by single digging or rotavating. Onions like firm soil and potash to grow well. I have to be careful when I am hoeing them because the growing skins are easily damaged, sometimes it is easier to hand weed between the plants. The main onion crop is harvested at the end of the summer. I choose a dry sunny day, and put most of the onions in slatted wooden trays for storing in a frost free place. Sometimes, just to preserve the tradition, I also make an onion string by twisting the tops of the onions around a strong piece of baling twine, then I hang them in the potting shed for everyone to see.

Sowing

Kelsae is started in a propagator, the seed is sown into an ordinary seed tray filled with multipurpose compost, then grown on in the heated greenhouse until they have reached the size of a pencil. They are then planted into the soil outside in mid march, about 6 inches apart, 12 inches between the rows.

Onion sets are planted when the daffodils in the garden are in full bloom. I space them out along the garden line before they are planted, then push them into the soil deep enough to stop birds pulling them out, so that the tops are just visable above soil level. The onion sets are planted out earlier than Kelsae at about 4 inches apart because they don't grow as big, but at the same distance between the rows as Kelsae, 12 inches.

I have never seen a blackbird pulling the onion sets out of the soil, but I have often had to push the onions back into the soil, they must wait until I leave the garden before making mischief! One year, I inspected the onion row and found that the onions had not only been pulled out but had completely disappeared. Could this have been a mouse who had a taste for onions? I never found out who the culprit was, there were no telltale footprints or any sign of the stolen onions, I just had to buy some more and start again, this time with a cover of wire netting. Such is the life of a gardener, something unexpected always happens!

Varieties grown
From seed the **Kelsae** for showing
Sets, **Centurion** and **Sturon** – these are minature onions
Red onion sets – **Hyred F1**

Peas

I don't grow many peas because they are time consuming to pick and the chefs in the café can't spend the time it takes to shell them. Still, I do grow an early variety called Kelvedon Wonder and also some sugar snap peas which are easier to prepare for cooking. Of course there is Mange Tout which is easy to grow and great to eat off the vine. There is, however, a problem with all of these plants. Mice love them. They love to eat the pea seeds. Before the cat arrived I had problems with disappearing sweet pea seed in the greenhouse. Now, however, they have realized that there is an undisturbed meal outside ... the garden peas. I asked Leon why the garden peas were not growing. Mice, was his reply. He said to get some traps. But I am soft hearted, so my method for growing peas is to start off the seeds in plastic rainwater gutters in the cold greenhouse. I line the gutters with compost, scatter the seeds onto the compost and they germinate in a very short time.

The air definitely has a different smell when spring is on it's way. All the birds are singing at the same time, and the sun is warming the soil. This is when I kick start the season by sowing some seeds outside, my usual list of seeds to sow begins with radish, spring onions, a few lettuce, parsnips, and a row of peas. If I sow the pea seed normally in the soil, they won't stay there for very long because they will be taken away and eaten by mice, so I have to try and outwit the mice. I have three choices;

1. Soaking the pea seeds overnight in enough paraffin to cover them.
2. Sowing in a length of rainwater guttering (not attached to a building!)
3. Sowing in the soil, then covering the seeds with plastic mesh, making sure that the sides of the mesh are weighed down to stop a mouse getting underneath. The protective covering is removed once the pea seeds have germinated, mice will not eat germinated seed.
4. Sowing normally.

To sow peas I use a spade to make a channel in the soil, using a garden line to keep it straight. What I am doing is making a wide seed drill the width of the spade, taking out 2 inches of soil. The peas are then thrown along the drill evenly. I wish that I could sow them evenly, but no matter how many times I have watched Leon sow them as he scatters them exactly, I still end up sprinkling a few at a time down the row. After the peas are sown, the soil is then raked back over them and patted down lightly with the rake to firm it. If the weather is warm and damp, the pea seeds quickly germinate. I water the seed drill before sowing if the soil is very dry.

Paraffin soaked seed can be sown in the normal way, the smell and taste of the paraffin stops the mice from eating the peas but doesn't affect the taste of the pods which eventually grow.

Sowing in a gutter

This is a very quick method to grow peas, they seem to germinate more easily in a length of plastic gutter. I have two lengths of gutter about 6feet long, I fix these above the ground in the cold greenhouse (about 4 feet high), and I scatter some peanuts on the ground to divert the mice. Multipurpose compost is used to three-quarter fill the gutters, and I lightly push the seeds into the compost, the most difficult part is transferring the young pea plants from the gutter into the soil. I definitely need help to do this; two drills are first made in the soil to correspond to the size of the gutters, one person has to hold the gutter (usually me), while the other person (Leon) guides the plants into the seed drill. The next step is to support the peas, because without support they will just flop over on to the ground.

I am very fortunate to have a small hazel coppice at the far end of the apple orchard which provides me with sticks not only for the peas, but the herbaceous border also has to be staked. I put on my warm gloves and taking a pruning saw (secateurs already in my pocket) walk through the apple orchard to the hazel coppice where I keep warm sawing lengths from the trees. The long straight branches are useful as tall plant supports, bean poles and for constructing garden benches, gates and whatever your imagination comes up with.

I've found that beech twigs are just as good. The hazel or beech twigs are cut to size and pushed into the ground next to the peas so that they can scramble up them.

Fortunately I have never had problems with birds stealing the peas but it is bad enough just having the mice!

Regularily picking the peas helps prolong cropping, this is a good excuse for me to eat a few straight from the plant as there is nothing like the taste of a fresh pod of peas.

Varieties grown
Early Onward and **Kelvedon Wonder** – **Sugar Anne** (mange tout – ie. edible pods)

Potatoes

I remember Leon once asking me to fetch a curf and mould up the spuds! I wasn't really sure what he wanted me to do until he explained that a curf is a large draw hoe and moulding is earthing up the potatoes. Later on he showed me his method of planting potatoes and I

still plant them as he taught me, but I plant the potatoes in my garden at home using an easier method.

I buy the early potatoes as soon as they are available, and I place them in wooden or plastic trays, each potato is carefully placed vertically, fat end upwards in the trays, this encourages them to sprout green shoots (and is called chitting). I position the trays on the greenhouse staging where there is plenty of daylight and it is warm. When each potato has sprouted, they are ready to be planted outside. During a dry spell in the winter, I dig a patch of ground over ready for the potatoes to be planted in early March. I don't plant them if the ground is frozen solid or very wet.

Tools needed for planting potatoes

A spade, a garden line for marking the rows, an iron rake, a wheelbarrow with as much farmyard manure as I can comfortably push, and some general purpose fertilizer. I carry the potatoes in the trays, and some short canes to mark the rows.

Leon's method of planting

I start by marking out the first row with the garden line. Using the line to keep the row straight, I dig out a trench to the depth of the spade (about a foot deep, this is called a spit).

    I then put in a layer of well-rotted muck to just cover the soil at the bottom of the trench. I push each potato into the muck with the fattest end upwards (as they were in the trays) and each potato is spaced about 9 inches from the next. I sprinkle some general purpose fertilizer called Rooster (pelleted chicken manure) on the soil that has been taken out of the trench, before I use an iron rake to rake all the soil back into the trench, completely covering the potatoes. The first row has now been planted and marked at each end with a short cane, working backwards from the first row so that I don't tread all over the potatoes I have just planted, I measure from the marking canes two of my feet, or 24 inches on a tape measure. I keep digging trenches and planting until all the potatoes have been planted out, and then give my back a rest!

An easier method of planting potatoes

Tools needed for planting – a garden line, iron rake and a trowel.

The preparation of the soil is the same as for Leon's method, but instead of digging a trench, the soil is raked roughly level. I then mark out the row with the garden line and put the potatoes on top of the soil in a row along the line, spacing them about 9 inches apart. Using a trowel, I move along the line planting the potatoes about 4 inches deep, remembering to leave enough space to allow for earthing up the potatoes later on.

    Before long the first green shoots appear above the ground. I don't know why but this always takes me by surprise, I head to the potting shed to fetch the curf and mould them up before the frost can damage the tender young leaves. Covering the growing potatoes with soil also stops any daylight reaching the tubers and making them turn green and inedible. When the first flowers open, this is a sign that the potatoes are ready to be harvested, the cuckoo will be calling and the aquilegias (grannies bonnet) in the Kitchen garden will be in full bloom. I carefully explore under a chosen plant with a small hand fork to see if the potatoes are the required size, if they are, I dig up a double-handful, and put them into a small basket, pick a fresh sprig of garden mint and proudly take them into the house for Mrs James. She is always the first person to taste the new potatoes, the very first potatoes of the season.

One day I noticed a man with a small girl watching me very intensely as I dug up a few new potatoes for the café. I felt a bit embarrassed at being watched so closely, then the man explained that his daughter had never seen where potatoes came from, she had only ever seen them in a Supermarket and was facinated that they came from underneath the soil. I secretly gave them a few to take home so that they could taste some real fresh potatoes!

Varieties grown
Arron Pilot
Duke of York
Winston (a good potato for the show bench)
Ratte
Nicola
The above varieties are tried and tested favourites, grown in the kitchen garden in a sheltered area at the base of the north wall.

Parsnips

I once made the mistake of sowing parsnip seed on a windy day. The seed is very fine and it blew away. Another mistake I made is sowing the seed too early in the year, as parsnips take a long time to germinate and all summer to grow to their full size. I have had to learn to be patient and wait until the soil warms up.

I have dug the area where the seeds are to be sown to a good depth during the winter, and removed all stones. No muck is added and the rotavator is used to break the soil to a fine deep tilth. All this preparation is needed to grow long straight parsnips and any obstacles in the soil will result in some interesting shapes, the most common are parsnips that are forked. Before sowing the seed it is a good idea to add a slow release fertilizer to the soil. I always choose a wind-free day and mark out the row with a line. Sometimes I sow the seed in a continous drill, thinning the young seedlings to eight inches apart, or I sow the seed in small groups of three or four seeds at a time. Then, when the seedlings have emerged I choose the strongest one and throw the rest away. The rows are about two feet apart.

I once did an experiment. I sowed some parsnip seed into plant modules hoping to get a head start when the weather was unfavourable, all the seed germinated quite quickly, but after they were transplanted into the soil the seedlings either died or failed to thrive, so now I know that it is hopeless to try and save any and they do have to be thrown away. During the autumn the tops of the parsnips will die back, making it difficult to find the rows, and I find it is a good idea to mark each row with a cane so that I can find them when they are ready to be harvested.

Varieties grown
Tender and True
Countess

Pumpkins, courgettes and butternut squash

There are several places within the Kitchen Garden where daffodils have been planted, they add a lovely splash of yellow after a long grey Winter. After the daffodils have finished flowering, I am left with a bare patch of ground, this is then covered with compost, mixed with a some well-rotted muck, to a depth of about a foot, into this the young courgettes, pumpkins and butternut squashes are planted. Courgettes will tolerate some shade, but the others need to be in full sun to ripen. The daffodils seem to benefit from this extra feed of compost, and produce more flowers the next year.

The seeds are all sown the same way, in a wide shallow pot and started off in the propagator, they are removed from the propagator when they have germinated. I wait until there are two strong leaves then gradually harden them off before planting out after all danger of frost is over. Some straw is spread underneath and around the plants to help conserve moisture and keep the Courgettes, Pumpkins and Squashes clean

I used to grow marrows, but soon discovered that courgettes grow rapidly, they can grow to marrow size almost overnight. Be careful when growing cucumbers, with this group the leaves are very similar to look at, and you could end up with pumpkins in the greenhouse and cucumbers outside.

Varieties grown
Courgette – **Ambassador f1** (dark green)
    – **Orelia f1** (golden yellow)
Pumpkin – **Orbit f1** perfect for Halloween and the smaller **Baby Bear**
Butternut squash – **Cobnut f1**

Swedes

For several years the Swedes that I grew didn't look as good as the ones pictured on the seed packet. I tried growing different varieties, including my namesake, but all I managed to produce were what are locally known as 'nisgals', small, stunted disappointing things. By chance I found a variety called 'Best of all' hoping it would live up to its name, and it did!

Home-grown Swedes don't grow to the size of footballs, if they grew that big the flavour wouldn't be as sweet. Swedes are members of the brassica family, and like all brassicas they sometimes have the top leaves attacked by flea beetles, which make holes in the leaves, slugs, active all year round (unlike snails who hibernate in winter), damage the roots if the ground is wet, otherwise they are easy to grow and there is nothing like mashed swede with butter and black pepper. Something I havn't tried, but I think I will, is digging up a few Swedes, cutting the tops off and planting them in a box of compost,placing them in a warm dark place (under the greenhouse staging would probably be a good place to put them) and apparently the Swedes grow new shoots. Because of the lack of natural light, the shoots stay pale instead of dark green and should be nice and tender to eat.

Growing Swedes

The soil Swedes are grown in should have been manured the previous year (to prevent misshapenness) sprinkle on some general fertilizer before raking the soil to a fine tilth, make a drill marking out the row with the garden line first, sow the seed about half an inch deep and cover back over with soil, then mark the row with a short length of cane so you know where it is and don't mistakenly rotavate it. These seedlings should be thinned to produce decent-sized Swedes to six inches apart, and the rows about twelve inches apart. I grow them for winter use to go with the Sunday roasts, and they will stay in the ground all winter because they are frost hardy.

Variety grown
Best of all

Spinach and Swiss Chard

One of the choices on the café menu is 'spinach roulade', a mixture of finely chopped spinach, mixed with eggs and flour, baked in the oven. It is filled with cooked mushrooms and leeks in a creamy sauce (or onions instead of leeks) then rolled up into a savoury version of a swiss roll. The roulade features on the menu all year round as a vegetarian option and it is a challenge for me to grow enough spinach to satisfy the demand in winter. Spinach grows quite happily during the summer months if it is regularly cut back and has enough water, but during the winter the growth slows right down and I have very little to take into the kitchen. Swiss Chard fills the gap, it tastes just like spinach when cooked and is easy to grow. I choose Silver Chard which, as its name suggests, has white stems. I also grow a variety with a mixture of red and orange stems called Bright Lights, but it isn't as vigorous as Silver Chard though very pretty.

Sowing

I sow Spinach and Swiss Chard (also known as Spinach Beet) directly into the soil in April, making the seed drill 1 inch deep. The seeds are sown thinly because I don't thin the seedlings out once they have germinated. Both these crops seem to be trouble free to grow. When the plants are small and the leaves tender I have to protect them from being nibbled by rabbits, as the plants mature the rabbits seem to leave them alone, probably because they would rather nibble on lettuce instead!

Varieties Grown
Bright Lights – has multicoloured stems and darker leaves.
Silver Chard – white stems will keep producing leaves all winter.
Perpetual Spinach – crops well all summer.

Tomatoes

If I had my choice I would grow just two tomato varieties; Shirley and Gardeners Delight. All problems with growing tomatoes centre round aphids.

Sometimes I cheat and buy four Shirley tomato plants from a local nursery because the temperature in the heated greenhouse isn't high enough to start the tomatoes early in February. But usually I start the seeds off in a heated propagator in March or early April, depending on the weather, because the tomato plants will die if they are exposed to frost, so they can't be planted out until the end of May. We have two heated propagators in the greenhouse. One is for the cat. Grow bags are a wonderful invention, portable and already filled with a balanced mixture of compost and nutrients. I have used them, but I have found that if they are allowed to dry out, they are very difficult to re-hydrate. I think using one bag stacked on top of another to give the tomato plants a deeper space to grow their roots is a good idea.

I was lucky enough to be given a number of plastic buckets about two feet deep. For several years I grew the tomatoes very successfully in them. I filled them with a layer of well rotted muck topped up with multipurpose compost and with some slow acting fertilizer added. They grew very well in these buckets. I also planted a few tagetes with them in each bucket to try and deter the white fly aphids. The tagetes are very pretty to look at with their bright orange flowers, but I still get sooty deposits on the ripe fruits caused by the aphids. This is an ongoing problem and one thing I have tried is hanging up yellow sticky fly-catching papers, but the sight of a bumble bee trapped by its legs puts me off using this method again. If the plants are strong and healthy they are more likely to overcome most attacks. This year I have prepared the soil in the cold greenhouse by digging in well rotted muck before the winter lettuce is planted out. When the lettuces have all been harvested I will add some blood, fish and bonemeal fertilizer to the soil and plant the young tomato plants into it. Each plant will have a cane to support it as they grow, and they will need a high potash liquid feed, which will help them to produce lots of fruit. Their laterals or side shoots will have to be removed so that all their energy isn't wasted. They can then concentrate on production.

Varieties grown
Here are just some of the other varieties I have grown.
Shirley
Cossack
Black Russian
Beefsteak
Gardeners Delight Cherry
Sweet Million Cherry

Pests

All sorts of problems challenge the gardener, it would be so much easier to grow things if they didn't get nibbled or pecked, lettuces have disappeared overnight, pea and bean seeds have failed, eaten by mice! I have a long list of disasters, but I have also learned how to cope with failure and have managed to grow crops despite everything.

Here are some of my methods.

Rabbits

A three foot high chicken wire fence surrounds the entire garden, it has been partly buried in the ground to try and stop rabbits burrowing underneath. Our rabbits must be very intelligent because I have witnessed a rabbit climbing the wire as if it were a ladder. I have to protect any plant that is young, green and tender with a hoop of chicken wire, or when the brassicas are planted out, the whole patch has to be fenced. Fortunately, rabbits seem to shy away from red lettuce so these can be left unprotected. Another thing that is a nuisance is they dig holes in freshly prepared seed beds, the beds have to be covered with pea sticks to try and put them off.

The only way to keep rabbit numbers down, is to persuade someone to shoot them at dusk preferably when I am not at work.

Our garden cat Denise catches a few young rabbits which helps, and frequently running a dog through the garden also helps.

Slugs and snails

I have two special helpers in the garden, a hen and cockerell. They are not as destructive as most breeds, maybe because they are cross-bred with a Buff Orpington. Both are quite tame and share our sandwiches during meal breaks. Because they are allowed to roam freely, slug pellets are banned. Gently scratching about among the plants, cleaning up slug and snail eggs is a great help, but there are a lot of slugs and snails around, especially after it has rained, so I use lengths of copper piping laid in a continuous line around any vunerable plants, the pipe must touch the ground so that snails cannot get underneath or in-between. The pipe gives the snails a mild electric shock, which, though it sounds unlikely, seems to work.

All the plants that are tempting to rabbits, slugs and snails are given a head start, seed is sown into plant modules instead of directly in the soil, and this way, the plants, when planted out, are larger than normal seedlings and are not as sweet and tasty to them. I always reserve a few plants in case of emergencies.

Mice

The surrounding stone walls in the kitchen garden are ideal for a mouse who wants to set up home, there are lots of suitable holes where it is nice and warm and dry with plenty of food to eat nearby.

Favourite meals are peas, beans and peanuts kept for feeding the birds. I have also discovered that mice like fish food, but what they don't like is the cat. All the mice edibles are stored next to the cat in the greenhouse, all the beans are also germinated next to the cat.

Growing peas outside is a challenge. How I outwit the mice is explained in the section on growing peas. I don't like the idea of usimg poison to kill mice, we once did this in the greenhouse before Denise arrived and for a long time there was the terrible smell of decaying mouse – we couldn't find where the body was. One wet day in the potting shed I heard a scrabbling noise underneath the bench, inside a large plastic bucket, unable to get out, were 6 baby mice. Of course, I had to release them away from the cat ... there are now generations of mice who owe their existance to my soft nature.

Whitefly

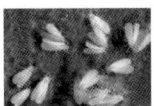

I have tried just about every method to get rid of whitefly in the greenhouse, chemical sprays, yellow fly paper, there is nothing worse than watching a bumble bee struggling to free it'self with it's feet stuck fast, tagetes have been planted underneath the tomatoes, and a visitor to the garden once recommended that I use fabric conditioner, it didn't work! Tomatoes can be grown with a certain amount of whitefly on the leaves, but the fruit eventually gets covered in sooty mould which has to be washed off as it looks unsightly. This is a difficult one to solve, and the first thing is to make sure the plants are in good health. I feed tomatoes regularity with a high potash liquid feed, I also grow insect friendly plants under the tomatoes, such as tagetes or poached egg plant. These will attract hoverflies and lacewings, these helpers are the reason why I don't disinfect the greenhouse after the crop has been cleared, but I do wash the glass and scrub off any mould on the woodwork. I have recently been experimenting with wormwood plants, they have a strong smell which could be a deterrent. I have yet to try them in with the tomatoes.

Deer

These lovely creatures are often seen on the Estate, fortunately they only occasionally venture into the garden, but one visit can be devastating. One morning I discovered that they had taken the tops out of two young apple trees, both trees had to be replaced. Roses are also a favourite nibble. But compared to rabbits and the damage they do, I enjoy seeing deer grazing in the distance without worrying too much.

Seasons

Autumn

The grape harvest is over, it's time to start tidying up the garden while the sun is still warm and the soil dry enough to walk on. I admire the surrounding autumn colours, highlighted against the pale blue sky as I cut down the herbaceous border, a robin perches on the rim of my wheelbarrow hoping for a free meal of worms. The leaves are beginning to fall from the copper beech tree onto the lawn overlooked by the kitchen window, no one really knows how old the copper beech is, but it would take the outstretched arms of three people to reach around its smooth grey trunk. All the fallen leaves have to be raked into heaps and wheelbarrowed

Denise, the garden cat, resting in the greenhouse

to the leaf mould pile where they eventually rot down and are returned to the soil as mulch. Tulip bulbs are planted with a Forget-me-not border in the triangle-shaped bed near the summerhouse.

The clocks are put back, and it takes me a week to adjust to the new time. It seems like a very long time until spring. There are fewer tourists now, the chatter of voices from people sitting at tables on the lawn outside the wine shop is replaced by the cawing of a solitary raven, and the cries of rooks above the pine trees. Butterflies flutter around the apple trees looking for windfalls in the long grass, shadows lengthen, the air is cooler in the late afternoon. I say goodbye to the swallows as they gather in a group on the electricity wires.

Most of the crops have been cleared from the kitchen garden; only leeks, brassicas, parsnips and swedes remain. There are also a few hardy lettuces growing in the cold greenhouse, and I have endive and radicchio planted outside, ready for the winter menu. Most of the flowers have faded or have been cut down for their winter rest, a few rain-blotched roses remain, reminding me of summmer when their perfume hung in the air for all to enjoy.

Winter

Climate change is more noticeable during the winter months. Most winter days now seem to be dark and damp. I squelch around in Wellington boots in the vineyard while I am pruning the vines. A bright sunny day is a bonus, buzzards circle in the cold blue sky above the vineyard, and in the garden frost sparkles on the lawns, cobwebs glisten in the sunlight, and at the end of the day I am amazed by a glowing orange sunset. But even on overcast days, the greyness is lifted when I see a flock of fieldfares fly over looking just like a shoal of fish, blackbirds cry pink, pink, pink in the hedgerow, and at dusk pheasants echo around the valleys and woodlands on the Estate.

Few visitors venture beyond the warmth of the café, so I have the garden all to myself. I realize that I must be one of the few

people who now spend winter working outside, and how lucky I am to be able to observe the subtle changes that turn winter into spring.

After Christmas the green shoots of snowdrops emerge followed by a lovely scented Mahonia shrub, planted under the pleached beech trees (approx. 25 ft tall, they look like a hedge on stilts) in the courtyard behind the house. I hear the repetitive sharp song of a great tit replacing the sweet melody of the robin who has kept me company in the garden.

In the valley below the garden, a row of tall poplar trees, originally planted to screen out the new houses built in the 1960s at Bodenham Moor, are among the first trees to break into leaf. There is an old Herefordshire saying, 'oak before ash, there will be a splash, ash before oak there will be a soak'. I can't recall the ash trees in the 'Break coppice', planted to shelter the field that is now the vinyard from north-east winds, ever coming into leaf before the oak trees planted next to them, is this another sign of a change in climate?

In early February a lone daffodil bravely blooms in the grass under the Horse chestnut trees at the side of the drive, there is always one daffodil which does this every year.

I sow lobelia seeds into trays and put them into the warm greenhouse to germinate. Potatoes will be ready to be planted outside in early March. I soon forget how cold my feet were and how the frost nipped at my fingers when the days lengthen and I can at last drive home in daylight.

Ironically, as I write this, I am unable to drive to work because we have had the heaviest snowfall for twenty years!

Spring

Underneath the apple trees in the orchard, along the side of the drive, everywhere I look daffodils are in bloom. Before the apple trees cautiously flower, buds break on the two quince trees planted beside the Cox's Orange Pippin and James Grieve apple trees, their pale green new leaves making a lovely contrast against the yellow daffs and darker green grass beneath.

Blackbirds sing a tune I once mistook for a melody whistled by someone walking in the garden. Sweet-scented primroses are found in the long grass near the rhododendrons. Leon shows me how to make a posy, carefully arranging the prettiest blooms in a bunch, circling them with their own leaves and securing the whole lot with a piece of green garden string. He explains how children would make a posy to take as a present for their teacher, gathering blooms as they walked along the country lanes to school. In the hedges, blackthorn has appeared first, frothy white and looking like snow, followed by scented damson blossom in the orchard, and pear blossom on the trees planted in an avenue on either side of the path leading from the summer house.

Everything needs doing at once, or, as they say around here, it's like being in a collander and not knowing which hole to come out of! I sow seeds into the sun-warmed soil, the potatoes are earthed up to protect them from a late frost, and behind me the bees are busy pollinating the pink blossom on the peach tree trained against the wall. The lawns are neatly edged, the lawnmower making a striped pattern as it mows the grass, and I inhale that wonderful smell of new mown grass, a smell that always lifts the spirits after the long winter days. On the other side of the Ha Ha, black and white dairy cows are turned out to graze the fresh sweet grass, raising their heads to watch as I push my wheelbarrow along the path under the pear trees. Fine sunny days bring more visitors of the human kind to the garden. An easter egg hunt is planned, and I make nests with sweet smelling hay in hidden places underneath bushes and at the foot of trees in the wild area where the primroses grow. I listen out for the first cuckoo echoing in the distance. May flowers fluff out the hawthorn hedges, a familier chattering is heard overhead, and there they are, the swallows, swooping over the garden and bringing with them a promise of long, hot, summer days.

Summer

I know that Summer has arrived when Denise, our garden cat, moves out of the propagater, to stretch out in the shade under a large potted pelargonium on the greenhouse staging. The greenhouse doors and vents are left open all day and if it is still warm when I leave to go home, all night too. I arrive at work with the sun already high in the sky, one hot day follows another, and the sun can be very helpful, burning off weeds as I hoe them, ripening the tomatoes and the peaches. But it can also be a demon, sapping all my energy so that I have to retreat into the shade provided by the yew hedges and the walls surrounding the Kitchen Garden. When strawberries were grown in-between the grapevines, we frequently had to hoe them, and it got very hot in the vineyard, the nearest tap being back in the garden. So I would carry a hoe in one hand and a bucket of water in the other. When the temperature got almost unbearable, I would stand in the bucket of lovely cool water, then soak my shirt in it and put it back on for instant relief from the heat. At least when I am working in the garden there is a tap nearby to drink from and a hose pipe to provide an instant shower!

The central fountain in the rose garden makes a cooling sound while I deadhead each fading flower. In the background I hear the sound of glasses clinking as cold drinks are served to people sitting under umbrellas on the lawn. All the surrounding corn fields are changing to a paler colour. I don't know why, but I always get emotional when I hear the combine harvester approaching. It travels down the track on the other side of the garden wall and I have the surreal sight of Keith's head moving above the wall as he drives past, sitting high up on the combine. I always wave and he waves back. Dust rises as the tractors haul in the corn, giant round bales sit in the emptied fields waiting to be collected. In the vineyard, grapes ripen from green to gold. Swallows swoop over the lawns, forecasting a welcome rain shower, which prompts every bird in existence to put on a concert as evening approaches. When I am watering the plants, from its perch in the pear tree at the centre of the garden a song thrush sings the most beautiful melody, my reward after a long hot day in the garden.

Leon tending grapevines in the polytunnel

Some recipes from the Court Café

Soups

Cream of Artichoke soup (serves 6)

Ingrediants
900g (2lbs) Jerusalem Artichokes
Salt
2 slices of lemon
25g (1oz) butter or margerine
1 medium sized onion, chopped
30 ml (2 level tablespoons) cornflour
450 ml (¾ pint) milk
15-30 ml (1–2 tablespoons) lemon juice
15-30 ml (1–2 tablespoons) chopped fresh parsley
60 ml (4 tablespoons) single cream (optional)
Pepper
Croutons to garnish

Method
1. Place the peeled artichokes in a large saucepan with 900ml (1½ pints) of cold salted water and the lemon slices. Bring to the boil, cover with a lid and simmer gently for 25 minutes until tender.

2. Drain the artichokes, reserving 600ml (1pint) of the cooking liquid, discard the lemon slices and mash the artichokes.

3. Melt the butter (or margerine) in a saucepan, add the chopped onion and cook for about 5 minutes until the onions are soft but not brown.

Remove the saucepan from the heat, stir in the cornflour and gradually add the cooking liquid from the artichokes and the milk.

4. Add the artichokes and bring to the boil while stirring the mixture, cook for 2–3 minutes.

5. Cool the soup slightly, then puree in a blender or food processor, or rub through a sieve. Return the puree to the rinsed out pan and stir in the lemon juice, parsley and cream, if used, and season with salt and pepper.

6. Reheat gently but do not boil, garnish with croutons and serve immediately.

Pumpkin Soup

Ingredients
(roughly chop)
5lbs Pumpkin
1 medium sized onion (skinned)
A 2inch piece of root ginger
2 cloves of garlic (peeled)

Method
1. Place all the above ingredients in a roasting tin with 4 tablespoons of olive oil
2. Roast in an oven Gas mark 5 (190°C) for 25–30 minutes until they are slightly browned
3. Season with salt and pepper and put roasted pumpkin etc into a blender with 1 and 3/4 pints of stock blend all the ingredients together.
4. Reheat gently and serve immediately.

Geraldine Smith   *Pam Morgan*

Savouries

Spinach Roulade

Ingredients for the Roulade
5 eggs separated (whites from yolks)
1lb (450 grms) washed un-cooked spinach or Swiss chard
1 tablespoon of mayonnaise
Pinch of salt and pepper
Ingredients for the filling
1 small onion finely chopped
½ lb (225 grms) finely chopped mushrooms
¼ oz (5 grms) butter for frying
½ teaspoon garlic salt
Salt and pepper

Ingredients for the sauce
½ pint (275 ml) milk
Corn flour to thicken sauce (about a heaped teaspoon)

Method for making the Roulade
1. Preheat the oven to Gas mark 4 (180°C)
2. Line and grease a swiss roll tin
3. Put the uncooked spinach, egg yolks, mayonnaise and a pinch of salt and pepper into a food processor and blitz for 3 minutes.
4. In a separate bowl whisk the egg whites until they form into stiff peaks.
5. Pour the spinach and egg yolk mixture slowly into the whisked egg whites, gently folding the egg whites into the blitzed spinach and egg yolks until it is all mixed together.
6. Pour the mixture into the prepared swiss roll tin and bake in the oven for 20–25 minutes or until the Roulade is spongy to the touch. Turn out onto a fresh piece of greaseproof paper, roll the Roulade up like a swiss roll while it is still warm and leave to cool.

The Filling
Melt the butter in a frying pan and cook the chopped onion and mushrooms adding the ½ tsp of garlic salt and a pinch of salt and pepper ,cook until tender ,allow to cool before pouring in ½ a pint of milk Return the pan to the heat and thicken the mixture with cornflour. Unroll the cooled Roulade and spread the sauce over the top and roll it back up as before, sprinkle the top with a little grated cheddar cheese, return the Roulade to the oven Gas mark 4 (180ºC) for 10 mins to brown the cheese.

The Roulade can be served with a fresh green salad (in season)or a tomato dressing

Tomato Dressing
Chopped tomatoes are put in a saucepan with a dash of Worcestershire sauce and some brown sugar and cooked until the sugar has melted, and the tomatoes are cooked.

Savoury Pancakes

Pancake Ingredients to make 10 pancakes
4oz (110g) plain flour
1 whole egg
½ pint of milk
Pinch of salt
1 heaped tablespoon chopped parsley

Method
1. Make a batter, sieve the plain flour and salt into a bowl, mix the egg and milk together with a balloon whisk, make a well in the center of the flour and gradually stir in the milk, egg mix until you have a smooth batter. Add the parsley and stir it into the batter so that it is well mixed in.
2. Pour some olive oil into a frying pan so that the oil just coats the pan, heat the oil and fry each pancake until nicely browned on both sides, allow the pancakes to cool before adding the filling.

Ingredients for the filling
1lb (450g) mushrooms ,sliced
6 medium sized leeks ,chopped into pieces
1 heaped teaspoon garlic salt
½ teaspoon black pepper
½ teaspoon salt
¼ pint white wine (Bodenham wine of course!)
1 dessertspoon cornflour
5 fluid oz (¼ pint milk)
½ pint double cream
10oz (275g) cheddar cheese

1. Heat some olive oil in a frying pan add the chopped leeks ,fry them until softened ,the mushrooms are now added and fryed until tender,pour the wine into the pan with the mushrooms and leeks allow to simmer for 5 minutes. Meanwhile mix the cornflour into the milk and gradually add to the wine, mushrooms and leeks stirring until the mixture thickens, transfer the cooked filling to each pancake rolling them up over the filling.Place the filled pancakes in individual oven proof dishes or one big dish as preferred. Pour the cream over each pancake then sprinkle some grated cheddar cheese over the top.
2. Reheat the pancakes in the oven (Gas mark 5)until the cheese is slightly brown and starts to bubble.The pancakes can be served with a salad or seasonal vegetables.

Pam and Geraldine's Vegetable Tart

A 9 inch flan dish is lined with short crust pastry, and baked 'blind' in the oven.

Filling
Slice the following:
Courgettes
Mushrooms
Peppers
Leeks or onions
Aubergines

Other Ingredients
4 oz (125 grams) cheddar cheese
3 whole eggs
¼ (137 ml) pint single cream

Method
Roast all the vegetables in olive oil until softened Gas 5 (190o C)
Arrange the cooked veg in the pastry case, scatter some grated cheddar cheese over the top of the roasted veg.
Beat 3 whole eggs with ¼ pint of single cream and pour over the veg and grated cheese.
Bake in an oven Gas 5 (190°C) until slightly browned on top.
Decorate with thinly sliced fresh tomatoes and sprinkle with some freshly chopped chives or parsley.
This recipe is a good way of using surplus courgettes.

Sweets

Short bread with Rosemary

Ingredients
15oz (400g) Plain flour
5 oz (150g) Castor sugar
10oz (275g) Margerine
A pinch of salt
3 sprigs of finely chopped Rosemary

A 5 inch x 10 inch greased baking tray

Method
Rub the margerine into the flour until it resembles fine breadcrumbs, add the sugar, salt and chopped rosemary, knead the mixture together into a dough, spread into the baking tray by hand. Prick the top with a fork and bake in the oven at Gas mark 4 (180°C) for 15–20 minutes. Sprinkle with sugar before allowing it to cool. Cut into finger shapes with a sharp knife.

Damson and Apple Crumble

Ingredients for filling
8oz (225 g)Damsons stones removed
8oz Bramley cooking apples peeled and cored
1 heaped tablespoon sugar

Method
Gently cook the prepared apples in a little water to soften them, but don't cook the damsons, put the cooked apples together with the damsons in an ovenproof dish, sprinkle the sugar over the top.

Ingredients for the crumble
6oz (150g) plain flour
3oz(75g) butter or margarine
2oz (50g) sugar

Method
In a mixing bowl add the butter or margarine to the flour (no need to sieve the flour)

Rub the fat into the flour until the mixture resembles fine breadcrumbs stir in the sugar,spoon the mixture over the fruit.Bake in the oven at Gas mark 4 (180ºC) for 30 minutes until the top is brown and the fruit tender.

Pear and Almond Tart

Ingredients for Sugar pastry
8oz (225g) plain flour
2oz (50g) castor sugar
5oz (150g) margerine or butter
1 whole egg
pinch of salt

A 9 inch flan tin

Ingredients for Filling
2oz (50g) self raising flour
2oz (50g) ground almonds
4oz (110g) butter
4oz (110g) castor sugar
2 whole eggs
1b (25g) pears peeled, cored and cut in half

Method for the Sugar pastry
1. Put the flour, castor sugar and a pinch of salt into a mixing bowl.
2. Rub the margarine or butter into the flour and sugar until it resembles fine breadcrumbs, gradually add the beaten egg to bind the mixture together.
3. Chill the pastry before rolling it out to line a 9inch flan dish, before baking it blind (placing greaseproof paper on top of the pastry to be cooked and putting some lentils or rice on it to stop the pastry rising or going soft) Gas mark 4 180°C for about 20 minutes.
4. Allow to cool before adding the filling.

Method for the Filling
1. Cream the sugar into the butter until it is light and fluffy, gradually beat in the eggs, sieve the flour and ground almonds together into a bowl then gradually add to the mixture. Pour the filling onto the prepared sugar pastry.
2. Drain the pear halves, arrange them artistically in the filling. Bake in the oven Gas mark 4(180°C) for 40-45 minutes or until the top has risen and turned golden brown.

The Gardener's Hymn

All things bright and beautiful, all creatures great and small,
All things wise and wonderful, the Lord God made them all.

But what we never mention; though gardeners know it's true,
Is when he made the goodies, he made the baddies too.

All things spray and swattable, disasters great and small,
All things paraquatable the Lord God made them all.

The greenfly on the roses, the maggots in the peas,
Manure that fills our noses, he also gave us these.

The fungus on the goose-gogs, the club root on the greens,
The slugs that eat the lettuce and chew the aubergines.

The drought that kills the fuchsias, the frost that nips the buds,
The rain the drowns the seedlings, the blight that hits the spuds.

The midges and mosquitoes, the nettles and the weeds,
The pigeons in the green stuff, the sparrows on the seeds.

The fly that gets the carrots, the wasp that east the plums,
How black the gardener's outlook, though green may be his thumb.

But still we gardeners labour, midst vegetables and flowers,
And pray what hits our neighbours, will somehow bypass ours,

All things bright and beautiful, all creatures great and small,
All things wise and wonderful, the Lord God made them ALL.

© Daloni Peel

Epilogue

A few years ago I found an old copper penny, dated 1901, when I was tidying the lawn edges under the pear trees. Finding the penny set me thinking about the past; and what the garden would have looked like at the turn of the century. I did some research and discovered an old map dated 1888. The garden then seemed to be mostly grass, shrubs and trees. Leon can remember in the 1960s an evergreen oak growing close to the house, and for several years we had a round flower bed where the stump was. The walled garden is plain to see on the map, it would have been a very important part of the garden, the only source of fresh vegetables, fruit and flowers. The gardeners employed to grow everything must have been quite important, an essential expense for the household for a key role. How lucky I am to be continuing to grow produce in a walled garden that is still used for the purpose it was designed for when many others have fallen into disuse. But now we rely on visitors to pay the wages!

Gardeners didn't have books or television programs to teach them how to grow things in those days, all the knowledge was handed down back then, and they had to save their own seed as well.

In the 1960s Leon welcomed the wonder drugs for the gardener. Chemicals were an easier solution, no more heavy wheelbarrows of muck to push, weeds were easily dealt with and sprays killed the damaging insects. It was the end of an era when he retired, ending a long history of gardeners who walked to work and went home at lunchtime. If, on a rare occasion, Leon was going to be late for work, he would borrow his daughter's chopper bike so that he was always first to arrive in the morning, and he rarely had a day off – the greenhouse had no one else to water the plants. Now we have come full circle, people prefer to know where the food that they eat comes from and that it is free from chemicals, so I am trying to grow crops almost as my predesessors did back in 1888. But I don't live on the Estate, and I rely on an automatic irrigator to water the green houses at the weekends. I wonder what the future holds, many young people now seem to want the glamour of celebrity gardening, they want to win a gold medal at Chelsea or become rich designing gardens. I wonder if anyone will continue to help preserve the old traditions.

As five o'clock approaches, I unload my wheelbarrow and put my gardening tools back in the potting shed. Then I collect my work bag and retrace my steps past the house as the sun fades behind the copper beech tree, on my way out shutting the gate to another day.